CAVEMAN APOLOGETICS

OG KEEP

Rock and Fire Press
Salinas, CA

Copyright © 2013 by Og Keep

Caveman Apologetics
By Og Keep

ISBN: 978-0-9862657-1-6

All Rights Reserved.

All rights reserved. No part of this book shall be reproduced, stored in a retrieval system, or transmitted by any means – electronic, mechanical, photocopying, recording, or otherwise – without written permission from the publisher. No patent liability is assumed with respect to the use of the information contained herein. Although every precaution has been taken in the preparation of this book, the publisher and author assume no responsibility for errors or omissions. Neither is any liability assumed for damages resulting from the use of the information contained herein.

SECOND EDITION OCTOBER 2014

Citation from
Excellence: Can We Be Equal and Excellent Too?
© 1961 by John W. Gardner
W.W. Norton & Company, Publisher
Used by Permission

Cover Design and Layout of the Second Edition
© 2014 by Maggie Pagratis of Custom-book-tique.com
Montreal, Canada

Library of Congress Catalog Number
TX 7-926-206
Registered as Og the Caveman

Rock and Fire Press
337 East Laurel Drive
Salinas, CA

Acknowledgements

This would have been impossible without the help of
Almighty God, to whom this work is dedicated (may it please Him);
A Canadian who read and commented on style and content;
A host of able teachers and writers who taught me;
A gaggle of atheists who argued with me;
And all who encouraged me.
Thank you one and all.

"Man is a little world, consisting of heaven and earth, soul and body."

-Matthew Henry, Commentary on the Whole Bible

CONTENTS

Introduction 1
A Precautionary Note 5
Chapter One 10
  Sound Exegesis, and What the Bible Really Says 10
Chapter Two 25
  Tools of Philosophy and Theology 25
Chapter Three 35
  A Practice Target 35
Chapter Four 46
  Subjectivity and Objectivity 46
Chapter Five 58
  Preparing the Ground 58
Chapter Six 64
  Arguments Against Christianity and Responses 64
Chapter Seven 113
  Atheistic Absurdities: When Argument Becomes Ridicule 113
Between Chapters; 117
  A Brief Moment to Rest Your Mind 117
Chapter Eight 119
  The Meaning of Life 119
Chapter Nine 130
  What Is an Atheist, Anyway? 130
Chapter Ten 134
  Common Misconceptions about 134
  God, Jesus, and Religion 134
Chapter Eleven 144

Other Arguments That You May Hear	144
Chapter Twelve	156
Atheism and Ethics	156
Chapter Thirteen	162
Order of Battle	162
Chapter Fourteen	175
Two Arguments That Are Like Atomic Bombs	175
Conclusion	187
So, Og, who are you, anyway?	187
Glossary	195
Appendix A	218
Syllogisms	218
Appendix B	222
An Outline of the Bible	222

INTRODUCTION

MANY PEOPLE ARE cowed by the very idea of theology and philosophy. They think it's a pursuit for "big minds" and not for the common man. It's true that a Philosopher or a Theologian will get more respect if he has enough letters after his name to obtain a good triple-word-score in Scrabble™, but are those letters really necessary?

After all, wisdom does not necessarily belong to the so-called wise. In Plato's Apologia, Socrates talks about how he tried to disprove an oracle. The oracle had said that no man was wiser than Socrates. Socrates tried to find a wiser man. He went to politicians, poets, singers, priests, warriors, and everyone else who was considered wise, but to his dismay, he found all of them to be foolish – the poets did not even understand the wisdom in their own songs.

Even a writer or philosopher who composes wise books may be a fool, a faker, or a conduit of wisdom from some other source. But because philosophy and theology use big words – *Sanctification, Ontological, Parsimonious,* and so forth – people are quick to write it off as a high-brow thing and consign it to the geniuses, even though a big word is just a little idea that's putting on airs.

To illustrate this idea of philosophy being out of reach, please consider something that John Gardner, the Secretary of Health,

Education, and Welfare under U.S. President Lyndon Johnson, said about plumbing and philosophy:

> The society which scorns excellence in plumbing as a humble activity and tolerates shoddiness in philosophy because it is an exalted activity will have neither good plumbing nor good philosophy: neither its pipes nor its theories will hold water.
>   -John W. Gardner,

Excellence: Can We Be Equal and Excellent Too? (1984, 1961) Published by W.W. Norton & Company, NYC; Used by permission

To build on this divide between plumbing and philosophy, there are two errors that we can make: the first is for the philosopher, as Gardner points out, to despise plumbing as humble and beneath him. The value of good plumbing becomes apparent when the bathroom floods. The second is for the plumber to console himself that he cannot recite the works of dead philosophers, but he can solder a water-tight joint; can the philosopher do that?

Many good plumbers are probably already good at reasoning, but don't know that they are, because they've never thought about it. They don't reason about the nature of the universe, perhaps, but they reason about why the clog at point A affects point B. It is second nature to them to know why pressure drops at point X but remains full-flow at point Y. The same skill which is used in troubleshooting applies also to reason.

That is why this is called "caveman" apologetics: We will approach the subject, not as reverent petitioners approaching a high tower, but as a mob of cavemen with clubs, beating the truth out of the woolly mammoth ideas. The ivory-tower types may not like this: It takes away their hiding places.

Some great philosophers actually raised important ideas – Socrates, for example – and I like to think that these sorts would have liked the competition. As someone once said, logic is a road upon which two may travel faster than one. Others, such as the Sophists whom Socrates so often confounded, would prefer that their empty arguments remain hidden from the common man. These folks do not want it revealed that the emperor has no clothes. These couch their ideas in lofty and obscure words, and "deconstruct essential existential postmodernism" instead of looking for the root of the idea that what we see is what we get.

So why not leave well-enough alone, and let the pretenders pretend, and allow the ivory-tower wise to continue their pursuit of whatever the heck it is they pursue? The answer is in Gardner's statement: We should not endorse nor condone shoddy philosophy simply because it is a lofty pursuit. We need excellence in our philosophy, just as we expect excellence in our piping.

How do we build excellence in piping? By setting out a host of competent plumbers, each seeking excellence in his own work. The shoddy plumber will be unable to find work, with so many competent competitors. By the same logic, a host of competent thinkers, each seeking excellence in his own thinking, will help to weed out shoddy reasoning. The multitudes will no longer be captured by silver tongues and gilt-edged words, if they can, themselves, reason; or at the very least, spot errors in reasoning when they see them.

This is why we need a mob of cavemen apologists, willing to give the Wizard of Oz and other such pretenders a good sharp analysis with metaphorical spears made of logic, and to enlighten dark corners with metaphorical torches of truth.

A PRECAUTIONARY NOTE

BEFORE WE DIVE IN, let's be clear about a few things. First, Apologetics isn't for everyone. I know that I just said that we need to get philosophy and theology out of the hands of a select few and into the hands of the ordinary person-on-the-street. But be careful about running up to the first Atheist you see, and laying out all that you know.

For some people, such as those who are more introverted and timid, or who have trouble in front of groups, a direct confrontation may not be the right style. These folks may find it better to use the material in this book to help them see the error in atheist thinking, but not to actually confront Atheists. Others may be able to confront Atheists, but lack the experience or the wisdom to see the argument through.

I would recommend, for example, that one not take an aggressive stance with Atheists until one has been a Christian for at least three years, and preferably five or more. The Apostle Paul reminds us that we do not all serve the same role in the body of Christ. "The eye cannot say to the hand, you are not an eye, so you are not a part of the body." Not everyone is an evangelist; not everyone is a singer; not everyone is a leader; not everyone is an apologist.

I would also recommend that a prospective apologist read as many books as possible, including *Know What You Believe*, by Paul E. Little, and *Mere Christianity,* by C. S. Lewis. Part and parcel of the Atheist's game is to try to trip you up, and many Atheists see no reason to be honest about it. Many of their arguments are based on half-truths (which are whole lies), and are specifically designed to shake the faith of a Christian who doesn't yet know his or her Bible well.

Christ cautioned us against preaching to those whose minds are closed. We are told not to cast our pearls before swine, lest the swine, having trampled our precious pearls into the mud, turn and attack us as well. You will meet some people who are not amenable to reason, and it will not be worthwhile to confront them. It is better, in some cases, to shake the dirt off of your sandals, and to walk away.

When I do confront such a person, in an internet chatroom or a discussion forum, I don't do it for that person, but for the third parties whom that person might influence and deceive. If I do make an impact on that Atheist himself, then so much the better. But my goal in those situations is to make clear to third parties that God has never been disproven – as some believe – and that the Christian faith is a reasonable faith, compatible with modern science and the 21st century world.

This sometimes leads an Atheist to try to use my faith against me, and when I was much younger in the faith, that might have worked. For example, Atheists sometimes react to an aggressive challenge by telling me that I'm shaming Christ, or not living up to what they think a Christian should be. But I am answerable to Christ alone, and to no others. An Internet Atheist does not get to tell me that I must be meek, or cannot challenge him when his position is simply wrong.

Don't misunderstand: Christians must be salt and light, and we should set a good example. But an Atheist does not get to hold up my Lord, my Faithful Friend, in whom the Atheist does not even believe, as a shield for his weak sophistries. Jesus is not a bogeyman, whom Atheists can use to rebuke us. We must know that we are justified by His Grace, and that only Christ can judge us – and even then, that we are covered in His Own Blood, shed for us. He is not seeking an excuse to condemn us, as the Atheist would have us believe.

Other Atheist tricks include pretending to want to convert, or pretending that they are a weak Christian, newly fallen from Grace. More often than not, those who say such things are deceivers, trying to get you to be gentle in your argument – to water down your words, and to make allowances for their aggressive attacks – so that they will have an advantage in the argument. This is where experience, discernment, and years in the Faith will help you. Listen to the Spirit, and see if what the person says really rings true. A tender heart will not throw sharp epithets at you; and a wavering faith does not throw up cut-n-paste arguments based on misunderstandings of the Bible.

A true seeker will present his arguments with respect, and will take the position of hearing what you are saying, without necessarily endorsing it. A false seeker will hint at being persuaded, but there will be scoffing, and an implied, "So there!" at the bottom of the gentle words. Sometimes, even an aggressive Atheist will say, "Pretend that you are trying to convert me." My answer is usually,

"Why? I'm not." This sounds callous, but we must face the fact that not everyone will be receptive to the Word.

Remember the parable of the sower, and the seed that fell onto the path, where the seed could not penetrate. The aggressive Atheist is like that hard ground. Your goal is not to convert the hardened Atheist, but to protect the weak Christian who is reading along, and the true seeker in the background, in whose heart the Word can find purchase.

If you do truly believe that the person you are debating wishes to know the plan of Salvation, present it in a simple form, and let them either accept it or reject it. It is not your responsibility to "save" someone, but merely to present the gospel. If you have done that, it is for them to make the choice to believe or to reject it. Again, discernment is vital.

Along with the pretense of being amenable to conversion, Atheists often use the ploy of asking, "Are you so arrogant that you believe your faith is true, and all others are wrong?" Quite simply, the correct response is, "Yes, I am EXACTLY that arrogant, and so are you." Anyone who believes anything at all is exactly that arrogant, since to believe anything – even that $2+2=4$ – requires rejecting all contrary beliefs.

In summary, know what you believe. Know your own theological position – that is, whether you believe in doctrines such as Original Sin, Transubstantiation, or Free Will – before getting into a discussion. One of the books mentioned earlier, *Know What You Believe,* by Paul E. Little, is a great guide to these doctrines. It makes the big words into easy concepts, suitable for us cavemen.

Also, be well rooted in the Word. I cannot count the number of times that an Atheist has started an argument by saying that the

Bible says this or that. The best response is always, "Where does it say that? Chapter and Verse, please." Now, obviously, to be able to call them on some of these absurd assertions requires knowing what the Bible does or does not say. As an example and exercise, please look up now where the Bible says, "The Lord moves in mysterious ways, His wonders to perform" (Hint: It's not in the Bible, but many people think that it's there somewhere).

Confronting Atheists, whether in person or over the internet, may not be God's plan for you, and that's okay. It is enough for you to learn to reason, both so that you can personally know God better, and also so that you do not fall into the snares that the scoffers lay for the innocent. As the Bible tells us, be subtle as a serpent, but innocent as a dove – It does say that, right?

CHAPTER ONE

Sound Exegesis, and What the Bible Really Says

THE FIRST KEY to sound exegesis is a sound relationship with God. Without the indwelling Spirit of God, you will read the words, but the message will escape you. And this is a bit counter-intuitive, because the Spirit is not a means to an end. We do not seek the Holy Spirit in order to understand the Bible: we read the Bible in hopes of knowing God and His Son, from whom the Spirit flows. C.S. Lewis once joked about those who think that the stairs of Heaven are a shortcut to the corner chemist's. We study Christ because He is our lifeblood; studying Him in order to be better at defending Christianity is like using the stairs of Heaven to get to the drugstore: it misses the point.

If your goal in reading the Bible is to prove a point, or to make a case, or to find a quotable quote, or to demonstrate that Noah's ark is a "metafictional metaphor," you're missing the point. For that matter, if you are trying to prove a point about history, astronomy, mathematics, or nuclear physics, you may be reading the wrong book. The Bible does mention many things, and some of them are so remarkable as to be noteworthy. But the Bible is not a math book, nor a history book, nor a book on astronomy. Where it touches these points, it does so in passing, as peripheral to the subject. The subject of the Bible is Jesus Christ.

Specifically, the Bible is about a relationship with Jesus Christ. Step one of sound exegesis is to know Him. That's not a means to an end; it is the ultimate end of all ends. Beginning a relationship with Jesus Christ begins by admitting that we are sinners. We all have sinned, and anyone who says that he has not sinned is lying.

We must also believe that Jesus Christ died for the sins of the world. And finally, we must claim His sacrificial atonement and confess that He is our Lord. Abraham believed God, and it was counted to him as righteousness: we find this in Genesis 15:6. We can be counted as righteous if we will do the same.

If you already have a relationship with Jesus Christ, it is important to remember that an intellectual knowledge of Jesus Christ is not the same as a personal relationship with Jesus Christ. Reading about Christ is not the same as spending time in prayer, or communing with God. To know Him is not just to know about Him. Read the Bible to know God, not to prove your point.

With that said, it is important to be able to put the Bible into perspective. Many people think that they know what the Bible is about, often because of a vague acquaintance with a few Bible stories and a couple of memorized verses.

The Bible is (to repeat it for emphasis) about Jesus Christ. It is a catalog of God's interactions with mankind. It has two major parts, commonly called the Old Testament and the New Testament. Jews reject the term "Old Testament" and instead refer to it as the Tanakh, or as "The Law, the Prophets, and the Writings." *

If we read the Bible as a story, the outline would be:

1. God created Mankind.
2. Mankind rebelled against God.
3. God began a long campaign to fix Mankind.
4. Mankind became progressively more evil, until God resolved to end the world and start over.
5. Noah found Grace in the eyes of the Lord.
6. Because Noah tried to be Godly, God rescued Noah's family (8 people) from the great flood.
7. After the flood, people began to repopulate the earth. Soon people spoke many different languages.
8. God began to work with one man, Abram (later called Abraham), and his family.
9. God led Abram to leave his home and to lead his clan across the desert to what is now Israel.
10. Even though Abraham was over 100 years old, and had no children, God promised that he would be the father of nations, and that his children would possess the land of Israel.
11. Abraham and his wife, Sarah, had a son, Isaac.**
12. Isaac had two sons, Jacob (Israel) and Esau.
13. Jacob had twelve sons by four wives. It is worthwhile to pay attention to their names and their birth-order.
14. Jacob's favorite son, Joseph, made the others jealous. They threw him into a well. Judah, one of the brothers, intended to rescue Joseph, but the others sold Joseph to a passing caravan, as a slave.
15. Joseph rose, by his merit and God's blessings, from a slave to the third ruler of Egypt.

16. In time, a famine struck the region. Only in Egypt, through Joseph's wisdom, was there any grain. Jacob sent his sons to Egypt to buy grain.

17. After first toying with his brothers, Joseph revealed his identity and forgave his brothers. The entire clan moved to Egypt, into the land of Goshen.

This is the end of Genesis; Exodus begins.

18. After 400+ years in Egypt, "There arose a Pharaoh who knew not Joseph." The Israelites became slaves.

19. God rose up a leader from the house of Levi, named Moses. He was a Jew, but was raised as the adopted nephew of the Pharaoh.

20. Moses killed an Egyptian for being cruel to a Hebrew slave. To escape trial for murder, he ran away into the desert.

21. In the desert, Moses married a Midianite woman, and began a new life.

22. One day, while herding sheep, Moses met God at a burning bush. God instructed Moses to free the Hebrews.***

23. Moses returned to Egypt and commanded Pharaoh to release the Hebrew people. Pharaoh refused.

24. God sent ten plagues upon Egypt to convince Pharaoh. The final plague was the death of the firstborn of Egypt, whether livestock or human. Only those houses that were marked with lamb's blood were spared. This is celebrated today as the "Passover."

25. Pharaoh let the Hebrews go, but quickly changed his mind and sent his armies after them.

26. God used Moses to part the Red Sea, allowing the Hebrews to cross on dry land to the other side. When the soldiers tried to chase them, the waters closed on the soldiers, drowning them all.

27. Moses led the people to Mount Sinai, where he had seen the burning bush. There, God gave the Ten Commandments.

28. As Moses led them from Mt. Sinai to the land God had promised Abraham, the people were often rebellious.

29. There was one tent, called the Tabernacle that was always in the center of the camp. It was where the people worshipped God. God hovered over the tent in the form of a sheltering cloud by day, and a pillar of fire by night. God's Presence was tangibly with them.

30. When they reached the edge of modern Israel, Moses sent twelve spies into the land.

31. Two spies reported that the land could be conquered with God's help. Ten spies reported that the people were giants, and would crush the Israelites.

32. The people were afraid, and refused to go forward. God ordered that they would wander in the desert until the present generation had all died, and the children were ready to go into the land.

33. Moses died, after being allowed to see the Promised Land, but he was not allowed to go into the land.

Here the Torah, or books of Law, also called the books of Moses, come to an end. Joshua, a book of History, begins.

34. Joshua led the New Generation to conquer – for the most part – the Promised Land.

35. After the conquest was largely complete, the people fell into a pattern of behavior: The people would sin against God. God would allow them to fall into oppression under a foreign people. The people would repent and cry out to God. God would send a deliverer, or "Judge." The deliverer would drive out the invaders, and lead Israel in righteousness. Then he would die, and the cycle would repeat. Samson was one of these judges.

36. The last Judge was a priest named Samuel. During Samuel's time as a judge, the people demanded to have a king, like the other nations.

37. God instructed Samuel to anoint Saul as the first King of Israel.

38. Saul began as a Godly king, but was soon corrupted. God rejected him, and ordered Samuel to anoint a new king, a shepherd boy named David.

39. In jealousy, Saul plotted David's death, but could never catch him to kill him.

40. Saul eventually died. David became King, and drove Israel's enemies out of its borders. This is viewed as a Golden Age for Israel.

41. David committed adultery with Bathsheba, and murdered her husband to cover it up. He then married her.

42. Because of this sin, there was always strife in David's house from then onwards.

43. David repented. The 51st Psalm is his confession to God.

44. When David was very old, he died. Solomon, a son of David by Bathsheba, became King.

45. Solomon was the wisest King, and expanded Israel's borders. He also amassed great wealth and married many women, as a form of political alliance.

46. Solomon built a great temple to God at Jerusalem. Solomon's Temple was the first of three temples to be built on that site.

47. Solomon's wives, many of whom were pagan, led him away from God, and involved him in idol worship.

48. After Solomon's death, the over-taxed kingdom fell apart.

49. Ten tribes from the North, collectively "Israel," broke away from the two Southern tribes of Judah and Benjamin, which were collectively known as "Judah."

50. Israel and Judah, at various times, were allies and enemies. They had separate lines of Kings, some of whom were Godly, but the trend was towards increasing sinfulness and idolatry.

51. In the sixth century BC, Israel had become so evil that God permitted it to be conquered by the Assyrian Empire. This was the Assyrian Captivity. These tribes intermarried with the Assyrians and others, and were thus lost to history as a distinct people.

52. The Assyrian empire was conquered in turn by the Babylonian Empire.

53. In the fifth century BC, Judah became so corrupt that God permitted the Babylonian empire to conquer Judah. This is the Babylonian Captivity.

54. The people of Judah did not intermarry with the Babylonians, and thus remained a distinct people. A Jewish

official in the court of Cyrus asked permission to return to Judah and to rebuild Jerusalem and the temple. This was the second of the three temples to be built on the Temple Mount.
55. This official, Nehemiah, along with a priest named Ezra and the remnant of the Jews remaining in Judah, rebuilt the city walls, hung new gates, and restored the temple.

This is where the Old Testament, or Tanakh, ends.

Chronologically, the rebuilding of the temple is the last event in the Old Testament, but the books are not arranged with an exact timeline order. They are actually arranged by type, and then by rough chronology. This makes a minor prophet, Malachi, the last book of the Old Testament, instead of Ezra or Nehemiah.

Between the Old Testament and the New Testament, there is a period of 400 years, known as the Silent Years. There are writings from this period, and some denominations include these as inspired scripture. These are collectively known as the Apochrypha. In general, most denominations feel that these writings, while instructive and useful, do not meet the standards of inspired scripture.

The New Testament begins at the beginning of the first century AD, with the birth of Jesus of Nazareth, who was given the title "Christ." "Christ" means "Anointed One" and is the Roman interpretation of the Hebrew word Messiah.

The story would continue this way:

1. Jesus Christ was born. He was not just a man: The gospel of John tells us that He was God in the flesh, and that to be near him was like being in the tabernacle where the Israelites worshipped, in the desert: God was Present (Immanuel).

2. He grew to be a man, and at about the age of thirty, began a ministry, teaching and healing the sick.

3. John the Baptist, Jesus' cousin, baptized Him.

4. Jesus began to heal the sick, the blind, and the lame. He chose 12 disciples and spends the next three years teaching them, every day and night.

5. Jesus made many prophecies about His own Resurrection, including that He will rise on the third day.

6. At about the age of 33, He was arrested by the Jews, and then sentenced to death as a blasphemer. The Jewish leaders convinced the Romans that He meant to cause an uprising against Rome.

7. Jesus was whipped nearly to death by the Romans, and then mocked and beaten. Still, the Jewish leaders demanded his death, so although He was innocent, He was crucified for the sins of Mankind.

8. One of the last things he said, "It is finished," signaled that God's long plan to redeem Mankind from our sins had reached its end.

9. At the moment of His death, the veil in the temple, between the Holy Place and the Holy of Holies, was torn in half from top to bottom. Any man may now approach the Mercy Seat of God.

10. He was taken down from the cross and buried in a borrowed tomb.

11. On the Third day, Jesus rose from the dead, and was seen by His disciples. As many as 500 people saw Him at one time.

12. Jesus ascended into Heaven, with a promise to return for those who love Him.

13. Fifty days after Passover, on a festival day called Pentecost, the followers of Jesus were gathered in a room. The Holy Spirit fell upon them, and they begin to speak in languages that they had never been taught. They preached the Death, Burial, and Resurrection of Jesus so emphatically and so clearly that 3000 people were converted to Christianity in that one day.

14. The church began to grow, and opposition began to mount. The leaders who had crucified Jesus tried to destroy the newly formed Church.

15. Many New Christians were disowned and shunned because of their faith. Wealthy Christians gave to support the poor Christians.

16. Deacons were appointed to see to the care of the poor. One of these, Stephen, preached to the Jewish Leaders and was stoned to death.

17. Peter was arrested for being a Christian, but an angel released him from prison.

18. Saul, a Jewish leader, was on his way to Damascus to arrest Christians hiding there, but was struck down on the road by a bright light.

19. Jesus spoke directly to Saul, admonishing him for ignoring Jesus. As a student of the Law, Saul should have known better.

20. Saul was blind for three days, but his sight was restored by a Christian in Damascus. Saul became a Christian.

21. Peter saw a Vision in which he was offered unclean food. When he refused it, he was told not to call unclean that which had been cleansed. Peter understood this to mean that the gospel was to be spread not only among Jews, but Gentiles also.

22. At that moment, messengers arrived from a Roman Centurion, asking Peter to come and preach to him. The Centurion, Cornelius, and his entire household, all became Christians.

23. Saul, the Jewish Leader who converted to Christianity, became known as Paul. Paul, and a man named Barnabus, began to go on missionary journeys across Turkey, Greece, and into Eastern Europe.

24. Later, Paul went on missions with a man named Silas, while Barnabus was accompanied by his nephew, John Mark, who later wrote the Gospel of Mark.

25. Much of the New Testament consists of letters from Paul to the churches that these men started.

26. John the disciple, sometimes called John the Elder, was sent into exile on an island called Patmos. There he saw a vision, called Revelation, Revelations, or The Apocalypse of John, in which details of the End of the World were revealed. It is emphasized, clearly, that Jesus will return at the End of Days, as a triumphant King.

This synopsis is not a substitute for reading the Bible yourself, of course. This is intended to give you a framework into which the other things you know about the Bible can be placed. It is meant to be the background that you need in order to understand the relationships between the various books and the events in each one.

Telling you that Christ, in the Book of Ruth, is represented as the Kinsman Redeemer, will give you an important point from that book. However, reading the Book of Ruth will teach you far more about God's redeeming love, and His mercy and grace, than I could ever do.

As you will have figured out by now, the Bible is a book of books. There are 66 small books which comprise the whole. Of these, 39 are the Old Testament, and 27 are the New Testament.

The order of the Old Testament books is by type, and then by a rough Chronology:

5 books of Law (Torah)
12 books of History (Holy Writings)
5 books of poetry (Holy Writings)
5 "Major" prophets ****
12 "Minor" prophets ****

Thus, the Law, the Prophets, and the Writings are, collectively, 39 books.

The New Testament consists of:

4 Gospels
1 History
13 Pauline Epistles (Letters by Paul)
8 General Epistles (Letters by other apostles)
1 "Major" Prophet ****

This forms 27 total books. And combined with the 39 in the Old Testament, that makes 66.

The New Testament is sometimes called "the New Covenant" based upon Jesus' statement at the last supper: "This cup is the new covenant written in my blood, which is poured out for you." (Luke 22:20). But the New Testament is also literally a covenant: It is the last message and the expression of the will of One who has died.

It describes how to treat the body of Christ.

It gives instructions to the heirs of Christ.

It gives bequests (gifts) to the heirs of Christ.

All of these elements of a will – a testament – come into effect because of the death of the Testator, namely, Jesus. Because He died, we have received the gifts of our inheritance from him, because of his will and testament.

One might contest whether the "Old Testament" should be called a testament – "Older Covenant" or "Tanakh" are often used when one is speaking with Jews, for example – but the New Testament, in addition to being a Newer Covenant, is also a Will. It is literally a testament.

Of course, we would be remiss if we did not point out that the will is even more powerful because the Testator, who died, also rose again from the grave. We have the best of both worlds: We have our inheritance and we have the source of that inheritance. We have the gifts of God, including both eternal life and the indwelling Holy Spirit.

We probably should not play word games with will, as in testament, and will, as in desires and intents. Still, it is interesting to note that when we wish to know the Will of God, we literally have it in writing, and we also have the Writer of that will living in our hearts.

---

* Tanakh is a form of an acronym for the Hebrew words meaning, "Law, Prophets, Writings." The Law (the first 5 books) is called the Torah. They are said to have been written by, or under the direction of, Moses himself.

** Abraham had a total of three sons who were significant in the Bible. Before Isaac was born, Abraham and Sarah decided to "help" God by giving Abraham a concubine (Sarah's handmaiden, Hagar). Hagar bore Abraham a son, named Ishmael. Also, after Sarah died, Abraham remarried to a woman named Keturah, and had a son named Midian (and other children).

Isaac is the son who was promised, and through whom God had intended to work out our Salvation.

*** Hebrew, Jew, and Israelite all refer to the same people, of course. "Israelite" literally means, "A son [descendent] of Jacob (a/k/a Israel)." "Hebrew" is thought to come from the Aramaic word "Habiru" meaning "rabble, hooligans, or rough mob." "Habiru" was a term of derision used by the Egyptians and others. However, Matthew Henry, the respected theologian, thought that the word "Hebrew" came from the great-grandson of Shem, named Eber (alternately: Heber), through whom Abraham was descended.

Heber was a righteous man, thus these righteous people are named for him.

"Jew" comes from "Judean," which is the Roman version of "Judah-ite" or "Judite (son of Judah)."

By the first century AD, there were only three distinct tribes (ten tribes lost their individual identities by intermarrying with the Assyrians, and were collectively known as "Samaritans" in Jesus' day – half-blood traitors, in the eyes of the Jews). Of these three tribes, Judah was the largest. Benjamin had been de facto annexed, and Levites (sons of Levi) had no land, but served in the Temple at Jerusalem, which was inside Judah ("Judea"). To the Romans, the people of "Judea," including Bejaminites and Levites, were all "Judeans" or "Jews."

**** The difference between a "Major" and a "Minor" prophet has nothing to do with the importance of their writings. Major prophets wrote longer books. Minor prophets wrote shorter ones. That's all.

CHAPTER TWO

Tools of Philosophy and Theology

LOGIC IS THE first tool. Many books have been written about Logic, and it invokes images of guys in togas, carrying lanterns and arguing about the essential substance of the universe. You might even envision a friendly alien on a space exploration program. Logic is actually much easier than that.

Just to be clear: there are a few types of logic, such as Boolean logic, symbolic logic, computational logic, and so forth. We will be dealing exclusively with philosophical logic, so you will not need any math books, and you won't have to think about operands and subsets. You won't even have to say "Fascinating," unless, of course, you find something truly fascinating. Or if you happen to be from a hot planet that orbits 80 Eridani.

Philosophical logic was formalized by Aristotle. He created a simple set of sentences that can be adapted to nearly anything that we know, to help us reach towards what we wish to know. This is called a "syllogism." It consists of three sentences, which are a "general premise," a "specific premise," and a conclusion.

The general premise is usually phrased as an if/then statement, such as "If today is Tuesday, then lunch will be spaghetti." This is our starting place, and a foundation for the rest of the argument. The specific premise will then tell us something more specific about the general premise, leading us to the conclusion. A syllogism might look like this:

> **General Premise:** If this is a Poodle, then it is a dog.
> **Specific Premise**: It is a Poodle.
> **Conclusion:** Thus, it is a dog.

The general premise will usually be in the form, ***If this, then that.*** We can think of it as a teeter-totter, with the fulcrum (the comma) at the middle. Our goal is to make the teeter-totter tilt to the right, which will give us the "right" conclusion.

To do this, in our specific premise, we can either affirm the left side –the "if"— pushing it upwards, or deny the right side – the "then" – pushing it downwards. Either of these tilt us to the right. But denying the "if" or affirming the "then" will tilt us the wrong way. That will mean a bad conclusion—no results, nothing can be concluded.

> If this is a poodle, then it is a dog;
> This is a poodle.

This specific premise affirms the "if," so the conclusion will make sense: It is a dog. We could also say,

> If this is a poodle, then it is a dog;
> It is not a dog.

This denies the "then" part, leaving us with an obvious conclusion: It is not a poodle. But if we say,

If this is a poodle, then it is a dog;
It is a dog.
Or
If this is a poodle, then it is a dog;
It is not a poodle.

We have said nothing at all. There is no conclusion to draw; the teeter-totter tilts the wrong way. Everything we know about the creature is summed up in the specific premise. So, as a general rule, if you get to the conclusion and say, "There's no obvious conclusion," the problem is likely to be that you're either saying "yes" to the "then" or saying "no" to the "if."

The other errors that we can make with a syllogism are that we can use a word to mean two different things – we call that "ambiguous definition" – or we can start with a false premise. Obviously, a syllogism will not lead us to the truth if the starting points are false.

As an example of ambiguous definition: if we use "dog" to mean a canine creature and also a metal piece that tightens a hatch, we will quickly run into problems. A poodle is a canine creature, but a poodle is not a metal piece that tightens a hatch.

Let's review the rules for syllogisms:
1.) Use each word to mean exactly one thing.
2.) Begin with two true statements.
3.) Make one statement into an "if/then" statement.

4.) Use the second statement to say "yes" to the "if" or "no" to the "then."

5.) Draw the obvious conclusion:

A.) If you said yes to the "if", then the "then" is also true; and

B.) If you said "no" to the "then," then the "if" is also false.

At first glance, it's a bit daunting. A lot of time and effort could be poured into trying to understand syllogistic logic. A good source for practice with syllogisms can be found in the Raymond Smullyan books, *What is the Name of This Book* and *The Lady or the Tiger?*, where the material is presented as a series of brain-teaser puzzles.

We will use syllogisms in this book, so hopefully they will begin to seem familiar by the end.

It's important to remember that nearly any argument can be "formalized" by placing it into a syllogistic form. Imagine a student coming to a teacher and saying, "I can't turn in my homework because the dog ate it." If we formalize the argument, it would look like this:

If I can't help that my homework is missing, you must excuse me;

I can't help that it's missing (because the dog ate it);

So you must excuse me.

The teacher will be a bit suspicious, of course. The first premise seems fair. We cannot punish someone for something that is beyond his control. But what about that second premise?

It might not be true, either that the dog ate the homework, or that the alleged meal was beyond the student's control. The student might have carelessly left the homework near the dog bowl, or might possibly have fed the homework to the dog rather than turn in an incomplete paper. The teacher has good reason to be incredulous.

And of course, if the second premise is false, the conclusion fails. The teacher does not need to excuse the student.

The Scientific Method

Another tool is a logical construction called "the scientific method." This is a five step process, whose origins are clouded in legend. The likely father of the scientific process is a medieval scholar and alchemist called Roger Bacon. He allegedly laid out five steps which can help us learn by experimenting. This is different from syllogistic logic, which is a purely mental exercise.

We might ask why it would be important to spell out how experiments work. The answer is that in setting up experiments, we may discover that they give us information that doesn't fit neatly into the question we wish to answer.

For example, suppose that we find a lamp that doesn't turn on when we flip the switch. We find a light bulb, so we swap the light bulb with the one on the lamp. It still doesn't light.

Does this mean that the light bulb we found is bad, also? Or was the lamp not plugged in? Or was the breaker tripped? Did we forget to pay the light bill?

This is how an experiment can go wrong. Changing the light bulb told us nothing. We know nothing that we didn't know from the beginning. We don't even know if the first light bulb was bad. Let's try it again with the scientific method.

First, we define the question: Why isn't the lamp on?

Second, we gather information: The lamp is plugged in, the breaker is turned on, and because other lamps work, we can surmise that the power bill has been paid.

Third, we form a hypothesis (an educated guess): Perhaps the light bulb is burned out.

Fourth, we test the hypothesis: We remove a lighted (known good) bulb from another lamp, and exchange it with the suspect bulb.

Fifth, we draw a conclusion: The light bulb did not light, so (with the other information from step 2) we conclude that the lamp is defective.

The big difference between our first scenario and our second is that we used a structured approach to spell out what we know and what we do not know. This way of thinking, forming and testing hypotheses, is the scientific method.

Informal Fallacies

There are several common errors in reasoning, which are also called fallacies. I cannot list all of the common fallacies, but each of them can be corrected by going back and fitting the argument into a syllogism. As an example, a common fallacy is to draw a specific conclusion from general information.

You might have heard the joke about the mother who said, "I was surprised that our fifth son wasn't Asian. We had read that every fifth child born in the world is Chinese." In this case, the general statistic (which may or may not be accurate) that 20% of all births occur to Chinese parents, does not apply to the specific case of an American family which is not of Chinese descent. The general information is not relevant to the specific question, and thus a wrong answer results.

Another fallacy is the false dichotomy. This is a "false split" or a "false division" of the facts. My father, an incurable kidder, used to be fond of asking, "Did you walk to work, or bring your lunch?"

The problem with this question (which usually caused a moment of confusion for the listener) is that it offers a false choice, by presenting only two of all the possibilities, and asking the listener to pick from between them. There are many other combinations possible, and the listener might have both walked and carried a lunch, or might have done neither one.

The distinction between a valid dichotomy ("cutting in two") and a false dichotomy is something called "the middle." The middle is "both" or "neither." If you are asked, "A or B," and the answer can be "both" or "neither," the middle is "unexcluded," and it is a false dichotomy. Also, if there is a third choice, then it is a false dichotomy. If the answer can't be "both" or "neither," it is a true dichotomy, and the middle is excluded.

So, did you walk to work, or bring your lunch, or both, or neither? Whichever it was, as my father also loved to remark, "Don't run off in the heat of the day without your blanket."

Kalaam Reasoning

It is sometimes useful to have a technique called Kalaam, which is an Islamic technique of discourse in which one forms and then analyzes dichotomies (splitting of cases, "dividing in two"). The general form of the discourse is "Either this or that; not this, thus that; if that, then this or that," and so forth.

The weakness of kalaam is that it can present "false dichotomies," as we just discussed, above. We may be lulled into analyzing only two of three or more options, or the options might have an "unexcluded middle."

Parsimony, or Occam's Razor

"Parsimony" (or stinginess) also often finds its way into logic. Parsimony is rooted in something alleged to have been said by William of Ockham (sometimes "Occam"). As with many attributed historical quotes, it is difficult to find the actual phrase in Ockham's writings, but he is often quoted as having said, "Do not multiply entities needlessly."

You may hear this phrase, "Do not multiply entities needlessly," referred to as "Ockham's Razor" or "Occam's Razor." You may also hear it summarized as, "The simplest answer is probably right." It is sometimes called "The law of parsimony" because it tells us to be stingy in making assumptions, but it is not a law in the sense of physical laws or "laws of nature."

Note that the word "Probably" must be used in the summary. The simplest answer is PROBABLY right. If we were to say that "The simplest answer is ALWAYS right," we'd be faced with all kinds of absurd contradictions. For example, the simplest answer to, "What is the sun?" might be, "The wheel of Apollo's chariot" or "A golden disk in a celestial forge."

The more complex, but correct, answer is that it is a large ball of hydrogen that is converting itself into helium using a process known as nuclear fusion. But the wheel of Apollo's chariot would probably be a more parsimonious answer, that is, requiring fewer "entities." Fusion is not required, nor the periodic table (a prerequisite to understanding fusion), nor the strong nuclear force, nor the weak nuclear force, nor quantum mechanics, nor Feynman's diagrams.

These only scratch the surface of the entities required in the "fusion" explanation of the sun, while Apollo's chariot requires Apollo, a chariot, and a couple of horses. If we are stingy (Parsimonious) with our entities, Apollo wins, hands down.

By contrast, if we are looking for the answer to the question, "Who took the last cookie?" then parsimony demands that we look for the child with crumbs on his shirt, instead of guessing that the goldfish was magically levitated to the cookie jar and back. In this case, Parsimony agrees with the most likely answer: A human cookie eater.

It would be more parsimonious to believe that the earth is the center of the universe, and that the sun and stars rotate around us than to believe in Heliocentricity, as yet another example. Direct observation suggests this very strongly. But it is false.

So parsimony alone will not lead us to the answer; it can, at best, suggest a direction. The best use of parsimony is as a method of deciding between two hypotheses. Still, we must use other tools to determine whether parsimony is pointing us to the right answer.

Hermeneutics and Exegesis

Last of all, we have hermeneutics and exegesis. Don't be put off by the words: Hermeneutics is just the set of rules that we use to make an exegesis, and an exegesis is what we draw out of a passage or book. Exegesis literally means, "pulled out." Obviously, a sound set of rules will help us pull out what the writer says, and unsound rules will let us get all sorts of silly notions that the writer didn't mean at all.

We need rules to tell us what we can justifiably pull out of a passage. One rule that I use is to assume a passage to be literal unless it is obviously figurative, metaphorical, or rhetorical.

For example, when Jesus speaks of a camel passing through the eye of a needle, this cannot be literal. The eye of a needle is much smaller than a camel. When Jesus speaks of a man with a beam sticking out of his eye, who is trying to help a man with a tiny speck of sawdust in his eye, the word-picture is clearly intended to be ridiculous. It was meant to tell us to fix our own problems before trying to fix others.

Another rule is not to guess at things that are not actually mentioned. If we add things to the story, then we are committing the fallacy of argument from silence: Because no one says that this is not true, it must therefore be true. That's bad thinking.

These are examples of rules for exegesis, drawing out meaning from a passage. A set of these rules would be called a method of hermeneutics.

CHAPTER THREE

A Practice Target

LET US SUPPOSE that we are presented with an idea that Australia does not exist. Australia, argues the speaker, is a mapmaker's joke from the 17th century, and Captain Cook turned it into an April Fool's joke which then became the conspiracy of all conspiracies.

Wait, you say. Apologetics is not about Australia, or conspiracy theories, or any such stuff; it is about Theology! We should be examining false ideas about God!

Excellent point, and we will certainly examine arguments for and against God, and weigh them for errors. But to start with, the Australia Conspiracy Theory is a paper target against which we can test our tools in a neutral setting, before we wander into the emotionally-charged realm of Apologetics proper.

So, let's look at each of these tools, and put the Australia Conspiracy Theory into perspective. I should mention, at this point, that I have nothing against Australia, nor Australians, but for the sake of this discussion, I must argue that you're all lying. Please know that I'm not serious at all; and Australians I've had the pleasure to meet have been great folks. All Antipodeans whom I've met, as a matter of fact, have been great folks – I say that so as not to slight the Kiwis, either.

Australia and Parsimony

Parsimony, as we said above, is stinginess in making assumptions. It tells us to look towards the answer with the fewest and simplest assumptions. In general, it looks for plausible answers.

To apply parsimony to Australia: Is it simpler to believe that we have been duped, time and again, by a huge group of conspirators, who have the power to control political leaders, air traffic, satellite imagery, world travel, atlases, and zoos? Or is it simpler to believe that the seventh continent is a really strange little slice of the planet?

Obviously, to believe that the seventh continent is a strange but real place is simpler, and thus Parsimony points to a real Australia. But this, as we said, is merely an analysis of what is probable, and many improbable things are actually true.

Parsimony could also be applied to suggest that Australia is not real. There are some aspects of Australia that are not the least bit parsimonious, such as the highly implausible voyages of Abel Tasman. In 1643 and 1644, he sailed completely around Australia, and discovered Tasmania, New Zealand, and the Tasman Sea. He did not report having discovered Australia, a tremendous trove of minerals and other treasures, even though the discovery and exploitation of new lands were an immense source of new wealth to explorers and their sponsors.

In this case, looking solely at the actions of Abel Tasman, Parsimony suggests that he did not discover Australia because it actually wasn't there. It is simpler – more plausible, more parsimonious, stingier with the assumptions – to believe that Tasman found nothing than to believe that Tasman failed to notice a huge hulking landmass, right in the middle of his route.

Parsimony leaves us in a dilemma. It is both more stingy and less stingy to believe in Australia. As we said earlier, Parsimony can only point us in the right direction. We need another tool to tell us the answer.

Australia and Kalaam

Kalaam, as we said earlier, is an ancient method of argument that examines a question by parsing it into two choices, and then eliminating one of the two. This has a built in flaw: We will talk later about something called "the unexcluded middle," which, in essence, says that there may be more than two choices.

Applied to Australia, a Kalaam argument might go like this:

Either Australia exists or it does not. If it does not exist, and there are people who say that they are from Australia, either they are lying or they are telling the truth. If they are telling the truth, then Australia is real. If they are not telling the truth, then Australia is not real.

Obviously this form of reasoning is not perfect, but it can be a useful tool. The "unexcluded middle" may apply – for example, people who say that they are from Australia may be telling the truth, or may be lying, or may be deluded, or may have been deceived. A simple Kalaam argument is not equipped to address each of these possibilities.

Australia and Common Informal Fallacies

To list all of the common informal fallacies of reasoning is beyond our scope, so we will only examine a few. Many of these fallacies have simple names and are seen often:

> *Appeal to the Emotions:* "Think of all those poor Australians who are heartbroken to be called liars!"
> *Appeal to Dubious Authority:* "My cousin has been there, so he ought to know!"
> *Appeal to Consequences:* "That would mean that Opossums are the only marsupials, and would you want to live in a world without marsupials?
> *The Straw Man:* "You're saying that our Astronauts were paid off, and I've seen their paychecks, and that's simply not so."
> *The Non Sequitur:* "So then Kiwis, I suppose, are a shoe polish company in the Bronx?"
> *Circular Reasoning:* "That opera house is in Sydney, and Sydney is in Australia, so that must be where the opera house is located."
> *Argument from Incredulity:* "I can't believe that there could be so large a conspiracy, so Australia's got to be real."

As you will quickly realize, each of these errors arises from a faulty reasoning process. For the most part, these errant arguments can be parried by asking oneself, "What does that mean to what we are discussing?" and "Is that really true?"

For example, in the Appeal to the Emotions shown above, does the idea that Australians may be heartbroken to be called liars demonstrate that therefore Australia exists? Obviously not. The two ideas are not logically related.

In the second example, the Appeal to Dubious Authority, does the cousin actually know? If we are assuming that so-called Australians have been duped or deluded, what prevents a traveler from also being duped or deluded? Also, how do we know he's not lying? So this appeal fails, as well.

Clearly, that the orders of marsupials would be reduced by 6/7ths – 6 out of 7 marsupials are found only in Australia – has nothing to do with whether or not the Opossum really is the only marsupial. If the others are false, they are false, whether we like it or not. Appeal to the Consequences does not help us.

As for whether astronauts were paid off – well, the original speaker did not say that, nor is it a necessary result of what he did say. This is a "straw man," which consists of incorrectly stating the opposing argument and then refuting the incorrectly-stated argument, and not the opponent's true argument.

As is clear here, the astronauts may or may not be "in on it;" and it is possible that they too have been hoodwinked, or that the speaker intends to say that they were subjected to a powerful delusion. Or he may say that the astronauts were blackmailed, or chose to keep the secret for patriotic reasons, or any of a thousand other explanations.

Another example of the Straw Man – and here we step into true apologetics for a second – is to respond to a profession of faith in God with, "And you probably believe in Santa Claus, also." (This carries the implied argument, "Santa Claus is not real, therefore God is not real"). Obviously, the argument is false, because Santa Claus is not necessary in order for one to believe in God, and even if he were – Nicholas of Myra was a real person, and fulfilled many of the tales that have arisen about him. The implied argument is not only poor logic, but factually incorrect as well.

The non sequitur is similar, in that it changes the subject. Non sequitur means "doesn't follow" or "out of sequence," and technically applies only to a logical argument that has a faulty conclusion. However, it is commonly used (as here) to refer to arguments that are simply nonsensical, or that have no bearing ("don't follow") on the discussion at hand. In our example, above, neither Kiwis (New Zealanders) nor the Bronx have anything to do with whether Australia is real or fictional. You may also see this called a "red herring," which is simply an irrelevant distraction.

Circular reasoning is the easiest error to miss. In circular reasoning, we take for granted the conclusion, in order to prove one of the premises. For example, if we are proving that Australia exists, and we say that the Opera house is in Sydney, and Sydney is in Australia, therefore Australia exists, we have assumed Australia to exist, or else Sydney and the alleged Opera House would not exist, either.

Many times, when we make a circular argument, we are also "begging the question," which does NOT mean that we are begging for someone to ASK a certain question. It means that we have assumed the answer ("begged") to the problem (the "question"). For most of our purposes, "begging the question" and "circular argument" can be used interchangeably.

Finally, what we can or cannot believe has nothing to do with what is real and what isn't. Many real things are quite incredible – just go read the argument about Schrodinger's Cat – and many credible things are fictional. We must be careful not to confuse what is plausible with what is real.

There are other logical blunders that occur often, but if you learn to spot these, above, you'll be well on the way to thinking more clearly. Note that each common logical error can also be exploded by testing it with simple syllogistic logic; If we fail to learn how to use *Reductio Ad Absurdum* (Reduction to absurdity), we are not fatally flawed as logicians. We can use the simplest tools, such as syllogisms, when the more complex cannot serve us.

Australia and the Scientific Method

The scientific method is merely a series of steps which help to clarify our thinking and to help us avoid errors. Most of the time, we use the scientific method without thinking about it, as a motorist uses the gearshift without necessarily reciting the H-pattern of the gearbox with every shift, but it is important to have the steps clearly in mind as we think a problem through. The steps are:

1. **Define the question** as precisely as possible.
2. **Gather information** about the question.
3. **Form a hypothesis** (an educated guess) based on the information.
4. **Test the hypothesis**.
5. **Either draw a conclusion**, or repeat the process.

Applying this to Australia, the question is: Does Australia Exist? We would then learn all that we can about Australia, and from this, form a hypothesis – that, yes, Australia exists, perhaps.

We would then test the hypothesis – our educated guess – by taking a sextant and a watch to Australia in a locked carry-on bag (locked, as a control against tampering; and carry-on, so that we can observe them at all times). The watch, compared against local solar noon (when shadows are observably shortest) will tell us our Longitude (how far we are from the time zone where we started). The sextant will let us shoot stars and learn our latitude (the angle to various heavenly bodies will tell us where we are with respect to the equator).

If our tests tell us that we are in the longitude and latitude where Australia is said to exist, then we draw the conclusion that we are in Australia, and that it is real. Otherwise, we draw the conclusion that we have been deceived, and we are somewhere else. This would not mean that Australia didn't exist, of course, but merely that we weren't there. We would then try to get to Australia by another means, and try these tests again – By sailboat, perhaps, so that we can control the course we set. This would let us repeat steps 4 and 5.

The scientific method has one flaw, and that is that we can be deceived through poor planning and improper controls. Dr. Richard Feynman, the famous Nobel Laureate and Caltech Professor, once gave a speech about what he called "Cargo Cult Science." He warned against making assumptions and taking things for granted, or repeating methods without thinking them through.

He remarked on a study, intended to prove that rats could be taught a certain trick. Instead, the study discovered the variables that must be accounted for in order to perfectly control the environment in order to make the study itself possible.

These variables – the things that could make an experiment give us a false result, are the dangers in the Scientific method. In our example above, we used a locked carry-on bag so that we would know that someone had not, for example, changed the time on our watch, and thus given us a false reading. But do we also need a control that proves that our watch did not lose time in transit? Or what shows that we correctly calibrated the time?

In general, the question to ask concerning controls is, "How do we know that this test will tell us X and not Y?" By eliminating the potential false answers, we (hopefully) narrow our results down to the correct answer.

Australia and Formal Logic

The best tool in the tool shed is formal logic. False ideas are most often presented as a torrent of words, with the assumptions and the logic concealed underneath. If we stop and reduce these floods to their simplest terms, setting them into the syllogism format that we discussed earlier, we can often find the missing assumption, the false step, and the outright lie.

As you will recall, the three steps are: A general premise (usually an "if / then" statement), a specific premise, and a conclusion that joins the two premises together.

It sounds difficult, but practice a few times and you'll discover that it's really not so bad. We are not used to formalizing what we say into precise little nuggets, but look what happens when you take a paragraph from an argument and formalize it:

"Australia is, without a doubt, the biggest conspiracy that man has ever seen, and proof of this is in the Duckbilled Platypus: Can you really believe in a venomous mammal that lays eggs, swims underwater, and has a bill like a duck?"

> **Premise:** If the Duckbilled Platypus is a silly creature, then Australia must be false;
> **Premise:** The Duckbilled Platypus is a silly creature,
> **Conclusion:** Therefore Australia isn't real.

The first premise is obviously false: Many silly creatures exist in places we know to be real. Consider the three-toed sloth, for example. So this breaks rule # 2, above. But let's ignore that. There are bigger problems here:

> **Premise:** If you can't believe in a creature, then it isn't real.
> **Premise:** Duckbilled Platypuses are incredible.
> **Conclusion:** therefore Duckbilled Platypuses aren't real.

In this case, the false premise – that incredible creatures can't exist – is not stated in the argument itself. It is only implied, and if you don't read carefully, you can gloss over it, as the speaker intended. Other implied, but false, premises are that a mammal cannot lay eggs (one, the platypus, does); that mammals cannot be venomous (one, the platypus, is); and that mammals cannot have bills like ducks (one, the platypus, does).

Formalizing the argument lets us take it step by step, and look for the mistakes.

So now then, my Caveman Apologist, you have the basic tools to reason with the high-brows: You have a spear, a torch, a club, and fire. With these, we can assault the citadels and high towers, and bring reason down to the ordinary man, where it belongs.

Let's leave Australia alone for a bit – Say, did you know that Abel Tasman sailed completely around it in 1643 without finding it? – and start to consider the meatier questions.

One Last Note on Australia

Something else that you may have noticed about Australia is that it is remarkably like the Christian Faith.

From where I sit, I cannot see, hear, or touch Australia, just as I cannot physically see, hear or touch God. I know of Australia by what I have been told by others, and through what I find written in books about Australia. In the same way, I know of God through the testimony of others, and through what is written in the Bible.

I could compose arguments against Australia all day long, but none of those arguments would change the fact that Australia is real, even if, for now, I know of it only by faith. So also, arguments against God – and we will examine those in Chapter 6 – do nothing to remove Him. My faith in Australia is virtually unshakable, as is my faith in God.

I know of God for more reasons than I know of Australia, of course. I have experienced God in my life, just as some people have experienced Australia in their lives.

Consider that to be food for thought.

CHAPTER FOUR

Subjectivity and Objectivity

ONE OF THE ISSUES that we face in arguing with Atheists is that they often wish to set the terms of the debate. They will make statements such as, "If God wants me to believe in Him, why doesn't He provide objective proof?" Jesus Himself answered this, in the parable of Lazarus and the Rich Man: "Even if One were to rise from the dead, still they would not believe."

An atheist will argue that because God does not consent to behave in a manner that is measurable and quantifiable, that therefore there is no evidence for God. But this is false. There is evidence for God – evidence that Jesus Christ lived, that He did miracles, that He died for the sins of Mankind, that He was the only Son of the Creator God.

When confronted with this evidence, the atheist will usually scoff. But as I say to them, ridicule is not a refutation. To make fun of the evidence and to choose to dismiss it without giving it due consideration is not the response of a seeker of truth; it is the response of a person who fears that his worldview may be built upon a foundation of sand.

The evidence for Jesus Christ requires a careful eye, but it is very powerful. It falls into several categories: There is historical evidence, there is the testimony of the Gospels, there is the fulfillment of scriptural prophecy, and there is the testimony of people now alive, such as yourself.

Historical Evidence

When we consider historical evidence, we must know our sources, and we must be able to establish certain things: First, that the source made the cited remark, second that the source has been cited correctly, third that the source would reasonably know whether the statement was true, and fourth that the source intended the statement to be read as a true and literal statement.

In the case of the first item, we may be mistaken as to the wording or the source of a quote. We may believe that the Bible says, "The Lord moves in mysterious ways, his wonders to perform."

The Bible does not say this. It fails on the first point. If we cite it, we will be called on it, and our argument will fail.

Another famous error of citation is the statement that Socrates claimed to be the wisest man alive. This fails on the second point, because in fact Socrates stated that he had been told by a friend of a statement by the Oracle at Delphi (thus Socrates made no such claim) and the actual statement was that no man was wiser than Socrates.

There is a difference between being the wisest man alive, and there being no wiser man. Socrates himself remarks on this error during his Apologia.

It should be obvious why a cited source should be a witness to the events he describes, since otherwise his testimony would be hearsay and rumor. Cicero made many libelous statements about Julius Caesar, for example, including statements about his sex life. But since Cicero could not have direct knowledge of Caesar's sex life, we should question his allegations.

Finally, suppose that we built an argument based upon a statement such as "I've told you a million times that..." – clearly, the speaker did not literally mean that he had said the statement a million times, and it would be dishonest of us to imply that he had.

The reason for these precautions becomes obvious when we try to use the argument that Flavius Josephus, an ancient Jewish historian, makes the following statement in his book, Antiquities of the Jews: "At this time, there lived a man, if man he may be called, for he worked miracles. He was the messiah."

It would appear that Josephus is stating that Jesus lived and performed miracles, and that He was God. We face a problem, however, in that some historians believe this citation to be an insertion by later writers.

Let us apply our four tests:

1. The cited book contains the cited statement.
2. Contextually, the citation does appear to mean what it is alleged to mean.
3. Josephus, writing at about 60-75 AD or later, may or may not have lived during the lifetime of Jesus Christ. If he did, he would have been a young man or a boy, and what he observed personally may be called into question. He did, however,

research his books, and thus could very well have found witnesses to the events of Jesus' life.

4. Here is where the question arises. If this were a later insertion, then Josephus certainly did not intend for this to be read as a literal statement; he would not have intended for it to be read at all. But if it is not an insertion, then he meant it literally, based on the context.

So to know what Josephus intended, we need a breakthrough of history, to reveal whether the passage is or is not a later insertion.

But stronger Historical evidence exists.

First, the New Testament itself is a historical source. Atheists are quick to write it off as a "holy book" and to accuse us of trying to use a circular argument ("The Bible says that the Bible is true, therefore the Bible is true"). But that is not what we are saying.

The New Testament consists of books written by people who were witnesses to Christ's life, and those books describe known historical events. This is unlike fables and old tales that begin, "Once upon a time." We are instead given historical touch-points: The decree from Caesar Augustus that the whole world should be taxed (the first census that was taken while Quirenius was governor), for example, pins down the date of Jesus Birth to a very small window.

The reigns of the various Herods (Herod the Great, Herod Antipas, Herod Agrippa, etc.) and the details given of their lives (that Antipas immorally married Herodias, for example); The governorships of Pontius Pilate, of Festus, and of Felix; The decree by Claudius that the Jews should be expelled from Rome because of the riots concerning one Chrestus ("Christ?"); All of these hint at specific timelines and verifiable details. This matching up of known events is called "External Consistency."

"External Consistency" just means that the New Testament sets its timeline in a known period, and matches known events – it is consistent with the external world. That alone does not prove that it is true; many works of historical fiction have been written. But it is an indicator, nonetheless. External consistency is something that we would expect of a true story. And the New Testament has it.

There is also internal consistency in the New Testament record. We can match up Luke's record, in the book of Acts, with the events described in the Pauline books. Paul writes to Timothy; Luke tells us who Timothy was and describes how Paul met him and mentored him. Paul writes of being in prison; Luke describes how he got there and what it signified. Paul pronounces a curse upon Demetrius the Silversmith; Luke describes the riot in Ephesus that led to this denunciation.

Internal consistency is, in fact, one of the most remarkable aspects of both the New Testament and the Old Testament. That so many books, by so many writers, could have one consistent theme and one consistent story boggles the mind.

Consider multi-book fictional constructs – Series of books about a detective, for example, or a series of science fiction movies. In order to avoid contradiction and errors, the writers must maintain exhaustive concordances of the details of the characters' lives. We cannot discover in book 23 that Fluella Mae Flunkenbush has never married, when book 17 mentioned her short but tragic marriage to the ill-fated Buford Z. Armadillo. Even a singular writer cannot maintain consistency across 66 books without a concordance to keep the details straight.

Critics and fans of book series love to find inconsistencies in the works of, say, Rex Stout: Was Nero Wolfe born in America, or in Montenegro? Or consider the inconsistencies in the works of Arthur Conan Doyle: What happened to Mary Marston Watson? Even with concordances, writers make errors.

The Bible writers had no such concordance to help them keep their story consistent, but their stories mesh; they are consistent over thousands of years. One does not need to keep one's story straight if one is telling the truth; there is no conflict in the truth.

Testimony of the Gospels

The gospels themselves are both historical evidence and sworn testimony. They pass the four tests that we described above:

1. They really do say that Jesus Christ is the Son of God,
2. They really mean it.
3. Two gospel writers (Matthew and John) were disciples of Jesus and eye-witnesses; the other two were associated with eye-witnesses (Mark with Peter; Luke with Paul and other apostles). They did have the means to know the truth.
4. They meant their writings to be taken literally and seriously.

So we have documents that claim that Jesus was the Son of God, written by people who had the means to know whether He was or was not. That is evidence in itself.

These documents agree. There are some minor points in which one tells the story of an event one way, and another slightly differently, but these differences serve to confirm that these are authentic recollections of real people. They didn't sit down, in other words, and try to get their story straight. They just told us what they remembered.

That is strong evidence.

Now, the argument here is not "The Bible says that the Bible is True." The argument here is, "These historical documents claim that Jesus was the Son of God, and these documents are testimony of eyewitnesses."

You can dismiss the testimony of eyewitnesses – atheists will usually, at this point, begin to point out that eyewitness testimony is the weakest form of testimony, and so forth. But eyewitness testimony is still evidence, and is admissible in court. Men have been convicted of crimes on the strength of eyewitnesses alone.

Fulfillment of Scriptural Prophecy

Here, again, detractors claim that we are attempting to use the Bible to prove the Bible. For this reason, we must make a distinction between the New Testament and the Old Testament.

Old Testament (or Tanakh) canon was closed well before the first century AD. In the first century BC, Hellenic Jews translated the Tanakh from Hebrew into Greek. Seventy-two rabbis independently translated, and then compiled their translations, giving us the Septaugint translation of the Old Testament. From this, we can clearly say, based on historical records, that the Old Testament was not changed in order to fit the New Testament.

Our argument then is not that "The Bible is true because the Bible says so" but that "The historical person, Jesus of Nazareth, was the Son of God because He could not otherwise have fulfilled the

Old Testament prophecies." The New Testament proves the Old Testament true and correct.

Examples of old testament prophecies include the year that he would be born. Daniel predicted Christ coming 483 years after Darius decreed that Nehemiah could rebuild the Jerusalem temple. That 483rd year is the same year that Caesar Augustus decreed that the whole known world should be taxed – the same year as the first census taken while Quirinius was governor.

Micah predicted that the messiah would be born in Bethlehem, the city of David. The Old Testament significance of this tiny village is remarkable – Rachel, Israel's favorite wife, died here giving birth to Benjamin. The Bible tells us that the Israelites cast lots for their portions of the land of Israel – see Joshua chapters 18 and 19 – but this city was in the portion that fell by lot to the tribe of Benjamin. The book of Ruth, the great love story of the Kinsman-Redeemer, happened here. And David, the great King of Israel's golden age, was born here, and tended flocks in these fields.

Jesus was born in Bethlehem, even though his parents lived in Nazareth, at the far end of the country. Why? Because a Roman Emperor, thousands of miles to the West, decreed that the whole world should be taxed. One must marvel at the workings of Providence, to place the right people – a married (but unconsummated) couple expecting a child – in Bethlehem, which was the right place, at the time when the child would be born, and when the 483rd year would expire.

To catalog the Old Testament prophecies fulfilled in the New Testament would be a work for a more patient and more diligent man than this writer, and others seem to have already done so – I refer the curious to *Evidence that Demands a Verdict* by Josh McDowell, and I would also encourage the curious to read his *More than a Carpenter*, as well. I warned you that you would need to read in order to be prepared for apologetics, and these two books fall into that category of books that must be read.

So History holds evidence of Jesus, Testimonies of the gospels hold evidence of Jesus, and Old Testament prophecies fulfilled in the New Testament hold evidence of Jesus. But a sincere seeker might still look at these and say, "Yes, that's evidence, but everything there can be explained. Perhaps we're just misreading it."

This brings us to the least controversial of all evidence: your own personal testimony. God is not asleep. He remains active in the lives of Christians. Minor miracles happen every day, and are often swept aside as coincidences and "strange lucky events." God is active, and He deserves the glory.

A Cautionary Note here: Be very careful what you share on the internet and with strangers. It is not necessarily wise to have your most precious gifts from God exposed to the laughter of scoffers and fools.

I know a man who was debating with an atheist, and mentioned a blessing from God: He and his wife were barren, and prayed for a child. God granted them a beautiful baby girl. A few years later, still medically unable to conceive, they tried again, and prayed for God's intervention. He blessed them with a second baby. This was done without in vitro or fertility drugs. He shared this story, only to have it dismissed as "pious coincidence" and mere happenstance.

Jesus warned us not to cast our pearls before swine, lest when they have trampled them into the mud, they might wound us also. This man's pearls – the miraculous answers to prayer that he sings to sleep at night – were trampled in the mud, and he was hurt by the callous dismissal of his precious treasures.

Beware of the world. They have no qualms about kicking us where it hurts. Be cautious about sharing your personal testimonies, and look to the Spirit to help you discern when and how to share the blessings of God upon your life.

With that said, I have shared a few testimonies of my own. One event that was very powerful to me happened like this:

I had a job that I hated. I liked the work, but the people I worked with made my job difficult and wearisome. I had applied for jobs at all the local businesses in my industry, including a new one that would be opening in the fall. Time and time again, I was rejected and overlooked.

Eventually, a crisis arose and I was fired from my job. I marshaled my savings and resources and found that I would be able to pay my bills for one month. After that, I would be completely out of money.

I was listening to a Christian radio station when they broadcast their daily Bible Verse: Behold the fowls of the air: for they sow not, neither do they reap, nor gather into barns; yet your Heavenly Father feedeth them. Are ye not much better than they? (Matt. 6:26). I had to acknowledge that the verse fit my circumstances, but I was still worried about the future.

I was teaching Sunday School at that time, and it was my duty to prepare the lesson. The other teacher would bring craft projects and games. I opened the study book to find that week's lesson. It was based on Matthew 6:26-29. I had to laugh.

Still, I knew that it was a simple coincidence. The verse just seemed more significant because of my own circumstances, and not because it was a message from God, right?

Weeks before, I had signed up for an overnight Men's Bible Retreat. We went to a campground in the mountains on Friday Night, and returned the next day after fellowship and worship together. That Friday night, as we sat in the lodge talking casually among ourselves, one of the men – his last name was even Bird! – spontaneously remarked, "You know, my favorite Bible verse is Matthew 6:26. I've always felt that it had a personal application for me."

How much clearer could it be? God was telling me, in no uncertain terms, to stop worrying – His hand was in this. At that moment, I gave the responsibility for my problems to God, confident that whatever happened – whether I got a new job or not; whether I went bankrupt or not – God would have his hand on the situation. God would take care of me. At last, I had peace.

A couple of weeks later, I got the job that I had hoped for at the new business that was opening. God was faithful. But the working conditions were so much better that it was a joy to go to work. Even better: When my new boss was transferred to another business, and needed an assistant, he called me, thus leading me into management.

The Lord promised to provide for me, and He fulfilled His promise.

Now, an atheist can write that all off as coincidence, and it won't hurt my feelings. I know that it was the hand of God – I was there, I felt His presence, I heard him speaking to me through the radio, the Bible Study, and the man named Bird. What others believe about it is their problem.

I think that this is the approach that we must take if we choose to share these pearls with the lost world. We must be willing to expose ourselves to their ridicule, and if this is not something you're comfortable doing, then it is best for you to find a less confrontational way to serve God and to further His kingdom. As for me, I realized many decades ago that I will always be ridiculed by someone. I made the choice, then, that I would be better off to be ridiculed for Christ's sake. For that reason, if someone chooses to laugh at me because I believe that God spoke to me through the radio – let him laugh.

Now, again, we face an issue here: MY strongest evidence for Christ – the evidence that convinces my heart and soul – is subjective evidence. It is evidence that I had to experience to truly believe. I cannot expect others to accept at face value that God spoke to me through a Bible verse, or that the fact that a man was named Bird meant that God promised me a job.

Their acceptance of that sort of evidence depends upon their acceptance of my trustworthiness. But what they do with the evidence, again, is their own problem. It is only my place to present the evidence.

An atheist will often say that there is no evidence for God. We have shown here that there is evidence for God, and that the atheist truly means, "There is no evidence for God that I, of my own free will, choose to accept." The evidence is what it is, and each man must decide what to do with it.

CHAPTER FIVE

Preparing the Ground

A FAMOUS CIVIL War general described his winning strategy very simply: "Be there first, with the most men." Today's verbal battles do not require manpower, but this principle – being prepared before the discussion begins – is still an excellent strategy.

Preparation can be divided into general preparation and specific preparation. General preparation begins with Bible study, and continues with reading. Know what you believe and why you believe it, know why your beliefs are reasonable, and know why you are certain of what you believe.

Reading – and a lot of it – is a big key to this step.

Begin with Bible Reading. I recommend reading the book of John first. It gives a clear and effective explanation of basic Christian doctrines and beliefs. Follow this with the book of Hebrews. Hebrews is tougher reading, but gives an excellent understanding of Christ's role as our once-forever High Priest. Next, the book of Romans, with Paul's clear and detailed explanation of the mechanics of Salvation, will give you a good foundational footing in doctrines. The book of Acts would be another great place to continue, and then First Corinthians, Luke, James, and Matthew.

Another good practice for Bible study is to find a topic, and trace it through the Bible. One possible tool for this is a Thompson Chain Reference Bible. This system uses four-digit numbers in the margins to refer you to a topical guide in the back of the Bible. For example, next to Exodus 40:20, which mentions the Mercy Seat of the Ark of the covenant, we find the Thompson's number 2303. In the index in the back, we find that 2303 is also next to six other verses. By reading these, we can learn what the mercy seat was, and why it was called the mercy seat. We also find a cross-reference, see also Holy of Holies, 1599 which can lead us to a further study.

We can also make a topical study or a word study of this sort by using an exhaustive concordance. One such concordance was composed by James Strong, who literally counted every word, including prepositions and articles, in the King James Version of the Bible. In case you're curious, there are about 750,000 words in the Bible. Strong's *Exhaustive Concordance* uses a four-digit number to designate the Hebrew word for words in the Old Testament, and a separate set of four-digit numbers for Greek words in the New Testament. By comparing these with the lexicon in the back, we can learn the fine nuances of meaning that a verse may hold.

As an example of such a study, I once had an atheist declare that no being, however transcendent, had a right to demand worship from another. This sort of egalitarian idea is absurd, of course. The way that a dog dances and leaps and wags in the presence of a human approaches worship, I hastily pointed out. They are amazed by our presence, and react accordingly. The atheist – well, a smirk is not visible on the internet, but I'm sure that he smirked. We do not demand that the dog dance and leap and wag. We merely accept it, and even discourage it at times. If we were to demand it, the dog would be morally justified in refusing, and even in being hostile towards us, he maintained.

I reject that premise on the face of it, of course. We make dogs behave according to our will, we make them serve us, and we make them defend us – all of which they do in exchange for the glorious experience of being in our presence and receiving our attention. But in order to truly put paid to this argument, I turned to an exhaustive concordance.

The concordance listed 100 Hebrew references to "Worship," 11 references in Aramaic, and 52 references in Greek. Of these, all of the references that could be read as a command from God referred to a word that means "Serve." For example, when God commands that Moses lead the people to Sinai, that they may "worship" him, the word used actually refers to "serving" God, and not to any sort of ecstatic expression of respect.

The atheist's response was that "that's not what Worship is!" That response has several obvious problems in it, such as the ambiguous definition of worship inherent in the response, and the clearly emotional nature of the statement. So as not to leave the subject dangling, it is necessary to explain the etymology of the word "Worship."

"Worship" comes from a Middle-English corruption of the word Worthship. The suffix "-ship" in this sort of construction refers to a state, such as "friendship," which is the state of being a friend, or "Lordship" which is the state of being an English nobleman. Worship thus is the state of being worthy.

When Thomas Mallory, who defined Arthurian legend with his twelfth-century work, *La Morte D'Artur*, told us that a knight was a "right worshipful" knight, he did not mean that the knight worshipped, nor that the knight was worshipped. He means us to understand that the knight was full of the state ("ship") of being worthy.

In Revelations, we find that the creatures before the Throne cry out, "Worthy, worthy is the Lamb that was slain." The Worship is in recognition of the worthiness of Jesus Christ to open the scroll. In Isaiah, when Isaiah describes seeing the throne room of God, in which the seraphim fly before the throne of God, crying out one to another that God is "Holy, Holy, Holy," it is easy to assume that these are just God's cheerleaders, and that this is their job. But when we read the passage carefully, we come to understand that they are crying out, one to another – That is to say, God's worthiness inspires them to cry out to each other in amazement.

So even if we were to grant the flawed initial premise (That it is immoral for one being, however transcendent, to demand worship of another) we still are faced with the fact that worship is merely an honest acknowledgement of a state of being: the state of being worthy of respect and praise. In such a light, the argument becomes absurd at first blush: It says, in effect, that it is immoral to ask that others respect us or acknowledge our worth. I doubt that anyone would endorse that argument, stated thusly.

We've mentioned the help to be found in Thompson's Chain References, and in Strong's *Exhaustive Concordance*. Commentaries are also invaluable in understanding a difficult passage. In chapter six, where we will examine arguments sometimes posed by Atheists, we will see how Matthew Henry's Commentary in particular was extremely helpful. Other good commentaries include *Cruden's Compact Commentary* and the Broadman Press Commentaries.

To be ready to study the Bible and to find the background of the terms in it is one way to prepare the ground before an argument. Another way is to read books about apologetics and theology.

I have previously mentioned *Know What You Believe*, by Paul E. Little, which clarifies many doctrinal points between Christian denominations. I highly recommend this book.

I also recommend literally any book that you can find by C.S. Lewis. *The Screwtape Letters*, *God in the Dock*, *Mere Christianity*, *Perelandra*, or *A Pilgrim's Regress*, all represent excellent examples of Lewis' work. You may find that his writings tend to echo thoughts that you have already had. I recently read *Till We Have Faces* for the first time, and found it to be an amazing work of apologetics in fiction. The Lord blessed Lewis with wisdom; we would do well to read it and learn.

I have also recently become a fan of G.K. Chesterton. His book, *The Everlasting Man*, played a role in the religious conversion of C.S. Lewis. It is a fantastic book, and will open your eyes to many spiritual things.

A fun way to learn logic is to work the logic puzzles found in Raymond Smullyan's *The Lady or the Tiger*, or *What is the Name of this Book?*

Surely You're Joking, Mr. Feynman!, by Nobel Laureate Richard Feynman, is another great book on reasoning, and is a fun read, although a couple of the essays pertain to Mr. Feynman's sexual exploits, making the book less than perfect as a guide to practice. It is the principles of reason in Feynman's essays to which I would draw your attentions.

Apologia, Plato's recollection of Socrates' trial, is tougher reading but well worth the effort. In Socrates we find a man who always wins his argument, mainly by questioning the underlying assumptions of his opponents. Socrates took nothing for granted, and we would do well to emulate him when we practice apologetics.

CHAPTER SIX

Arguments Against Christianity and Responses

THERE ARE VARIOUS arguments that are used against Christianity, and some of them sound reasonable if they are not examined critically. It is not uncommon for Christians and those who are sincerely seeking spiritual truth to be confused by these arguments, and even led astray. Each argument will be stated simply but sincerely, so that we are not arguing against straw men.

Arguments that we will examine here include these:

> Could God create a rock so huge that He could not lift it?
> Hasn't Science disproved all that stuff?
> Can God be both benevolent and omnipotent?
> Can God be "four-Omni?"
> Why would a loving God allow X?
> Why would a loving God do X?
> Doesn't God's foreknowledge make us predestined to fail?
> Isn't the God hypothesis "not falsifiable," and thus useless?
> Does Evolution disprove God?
> Isn't God old-fashioned?

Didn't man create God?
Are you really so arrogant as to believe that your version of God is true and correct, and all others are false?
Which version of Christianity is really true?
Which Bible is the right one?
Doesn't the Bible contain errors and contradictions?
How could they make a fire 7 times hotter?
Isn't Pascal's Wager for Wimps?
Isn't that just a God-of-the-Gaps argument?
Why hasn't God made more of an effort to make Himself obvious to Me, personally?
Isn't God Unscientific?
Jesus Christ was not "The Best and Wisest of men" because He cursed a fig tree.
How do we know that God is "Good?"
Iron Chariots? Seriously?
So, which god is God, anyway?
How can one being, however transcendent, demand that another being worship Him?
Wasn't the Catholic church mean to Galileo?
If you weren't raised Christian, you wouldn't be one now.
What about Cognitive Biases?
What about Russell's Teapot?

In no particular order, let's examine these arguments.

Could God create a rock so huge that He could not lift it?
Questions of this type are referred to in logic as "Improper Questions." These questions are not improper in the sense of

social propriety – that is, they are not wrong for being rude – but they are logically improper, because they assume two or more contradictory premises.

In the case of this specific question, God's omnipotence is assumed, and it is also assumed that there exists a size of rock which would be beyond the limits of His omnipotence. These are mutually contradictory premises:

P1: God can do anything
P2: There could exist a rock God couldn't move.

Lest anyone should think that this is merely a technicality, let's pretend that it is a sensible question, properly put, and answer it theologically. We know that God can choose to limit Himself, if He so chooses. We find in Philippians that Jesus laid aside His glory for a time, during His Incarnation. We find throughout the Bible that God chooses to avoid certain actions under certain conditions, as when He agrees to spare Sodom for the sake of ten righteous men.

So it should be obvious that God could choose to limit Himself by choosing never to lift a rock that He had created. But that's not what the asking party usually intends to suggest, and given this answer, will likely say, "That's not what I meant." The suggestion is that God might deliberately make a rock, but accidentally cause it to be larger than He is capable of lifting, regardless of whether He chose to do so. It should be clear that ambiguous definition plays a role here.

Obviously, one thing badly defined is what the question means by "could not lift," which might mean "Chose to never lift" (i.e. "could not" by virtue of a self-imposed rule) or "is incapable of lifting" (i.e "Could Not" by virtue of lacking the capacity to do so). The distinction is large enough to sway the answer; if we use the former, the answer is Yes, and if the latter, it is no.

So even if the question was logically proper, it still would not make sense. This is a nonsensical argument.

Hasn't Science disproved all that stuff?

Science cannot disprove theological matters. Miracles, for example, are suspensions of the physical laws. If a physical law is suspended, it cannot be used to disprove the miracle.

Consider the miracle of the Water and Wine. Natural physical law leads us to believe that water cannot naturally turn into wine. Therefore if water turned into wine, the event was supernatural; if the events were natural, then water did not turn into wine. And there deduction stops us. Since it is given that it was a supernatural event, it is irrelevant that it cannot happen naturally. In order to go further, we must either assume that the water did become wine, or assume that it did not.

"Science" – by which we usually mean deductive reasoning – cannot help us to answer the question.

Can God be both benevolent and omnipotent?

If we were to formalize this question, it would appear something like this:

P1: An omnipotent God could prevent any evil from befalling any person.

P2: A benevolent God would prevent any evil from befalling any person.
P3: Evil befalls some people.
Conclusion: Therefore God cannot be both Benevolent and omnipotent.

The second premise, P2, is the first issue. The mistake here is to assume that God's benevolence – Benevolence means "Good Will" – is absolute. Some versions of this argument will use the word "Omni-benevolent," meaning that God is "All-good-willed" or "perfectly good-willed." However, according to the Bible, it is not God's first intention to make us happy, but to make us Godly.

If, by "benevolent" we mean that God has our best interest at heart, then we can call Him benevolent. A dentist has our best interest at heart, and yet causes us pain, but the fault is not his. He has done everything possible to reduce the pain. The fault lies with us.

We are flawed: we have the curse of Adam, which is that we are drawn towards sin. To remove this from us, God allows us to be abraded by pain. It is a necessary step in our sanctification – our slow process of becoming Godly.

So long as we understand this definition of benevolence, and do not assume that it means that nothing bad will ever happen to us, then we can answer decisively: Yes, God is both omnipotent and benevolent.

This question, and its restatement in the next question, are known as the "Problem of Evil." Answers to the Problem of Evil are called Theodicies, based upon the title of a book by a French

Theologian, in which he answered the problem of evil by saying that Free Will requires that evil be possible.

Can God be "Four-Omni?"

This is a continuation of the prior question. The "four-omnis" are Omnipotence (to be all-powerful), Omniscience (to be all-knowing), Omnipresence (to be present everywhere), and Omnibenevolence (to be perfectly good-willed). One should note that the term "Omnibenevolent" is a relatively new invention, and will not be found in most lexicons. It appears in a few theological works within the last two centuries, but is generally not used. It seems redundant, as there is little or no distinction between benevolence and omnibenevolence.

As we discussed in the prior question, above, this question requires that we clearly define "benevolent," but expands the argument to also argue that if God is omniscient, then his foreknowledge that Mankind would sin should have prevented Him from creating Mankind. This pits His benevolence against His omniscience, where the former question specifically pitted His omnipotence against His benevolence.

Again, the assumption that God's intent is to make humans happy, vice Godly, forms the root of this problem. In Jeremiah, the Bible specifically points out that it is within a potter's right to make two dishes from the same clay, and to use one for a good purpose – perhaps as a decorative vessel – and another for a base purpose – a dog's dish, perhaps. We would not have the dog dish complain that the potter was not benevolent; in fact, the potter made a useful item from an amorphous lump of mud. That the potter also made something better of another lump is not relevant.

Thus, it is God's right to make humans, knowing that they will fall, and that some will be damned. That does not change the fact that He is good-willed towards those humans: The Bible tells us that God is not willing that any should perish, but that all should come to repentance. For God to have made us shows sufficient good will. For Him to redeem us also is good will beyond measure.

There are other theological opinions on this matter. One theologian took the position that this is the "Best of all possible worlds" and that for God to have created humans in any other way, or for God not to have created humans at all, would necessarily have caused a greater evil and still more pain and suffering.

Whether this latter view is correct or not, it should be clear that we do not know God's mind, nor do we know what considerations went into His choices. But so long as we define benevolence correctly, we can be confident that God knows all, can do all, and is in all places; with our best interests at heart.

Is God Good or is Good God?

This question stems from a Socratic dialog. Plato records a discussion between Euthyphro and Socrates. Euthyphro proposed to report his father for a cruel act against a servant. Socrates argued that to do so would be impious towards his father, violating "filial piety." This then leads them into a logical conundrum of why some things are considered pious – is it because they are a rule from a god, or is it because they are a rule which even the gods must acknowledge?

You may hear this spoken of as "the Euthyphro Dilemma." Usually, however, someone who invokes this dilemma will have substituted "good" for "pious" and "God" for "gods." They may or may not know that there is a distinction.

The modernized version of this dilemma asks why we call God "good" and precisely what we mean by it. Logically, if God is good because there is a standard above God, by which He may be judged to be good or not-good, then God is not the ultimate judge and the highest being. There would have to be something above Him.

On the other hand, if we say that goodness is to match the attributes of God, or that goodness is to follow God's instruction, then what does it mean to say that God is good? Goodness then is entirely arbitrary.

When I say that God is good, that is to say that God reflects and epitomizes those attributes which He has taught us to value. He commands that we be merciful, and He is merciful; He commands that we love justice, and He is just. This makes the statement reflexive.

We could as well say, "God is as God is." It turns out that this view of God is a correct statement: God identified Himself to Moses as, "I Am that I Am." It is a small step to say that He also is as He is.

This will often lead one's opponent to ask about some heinous crime, and to say, "If your God commanded you to do [insert evil deed here] would you do it?" The only logical answer is, "If that were what God considered Good, then I would not know any better, just as a fish does not know that it is wet."

Note, if you please, that this last question is another improper question (as with God making a rock too big to move). In this case, the mutually contradictory assumptions are, first, that our God makes the command (whom we know to be good) and, secondly, that God commands the evil action: That God is the God we know, and also is a completely different God. If God were evil, we would not know that the evil action was evil – Our lens on good and evil would be based on the malevolent God's definition of Good.

The response will likely be, "But you DO know that it's evil. Would you do it?" which compounds the contradictory assumptions. This time, it assumes a universe in which I know that a thing is evil – meaning that it is contrary to what God commands and the nature of God – and in which God commands such a deed, and in which it is not contrary to His nature.

This sort of an argument "plays both ends against the middle." The goal of your opponent is to create a dilemma in which neither choice is consistent with there being a God. The argument is entirely smoke and mirrors: It hinges upon contradictory assumptions.

But God is good. He is as advertised, and the things He does are the epitome of goodness. He demonstrates those attributes that He desires that we value.

One other note on old Euthyphyro: If we examine the original question as Socrates asked it of Euthyphyro, we note that Socrates is, in effect, saying that there must be something spiritually deeper than the gods of 5th century Greece. He is in fact pointing out the inadequacy of the religious system of his day, and implying a deeper set of rules – and with them a single, eternal God.

Why would a loving God allow X?

This argument, before we even examine it, already has the problem of assuming that we can look into God's mind and analyze His thoughts. It is, at best, an argument from ignorance: I do not know why God would do X, therefore God did not do X (or should not do X). For this to make any sense at all, we would have to be omniscient. But ignoring this fatal flaw:

Earlier we used the example of a dentist to show that a person can have good will and still cause us pain. We might as well ask, "Why would a loving dentist allow us to endure a root canal?" or "Why would a loving doctor perform an appendectomy?" We must not confuse love – which is to desire what is best for the one who is loved – with the pursuit of happiness.

A counter-argument sometimes posed by atheists is that God had the power to make our teeth perfect without the dentist's drill, therefore that He did not do so shows that either He is powerless or that He does not care. But we have already discussed how it is not God's purpose to make us happy or to spare us pain (those are merely byproducts) but to make us godly. It therefore may not have been in our best interests to have had perfect teeth, and to say otherwise is necessarily an argument from silence.

Why would a loving God do X?

This argument is a carbon copy of the one above, except that God's role changes from passive (allowing an evil to happen) to active (causing an evil to happen). An example of this form of argument is the question: "How could a loving God reject one of His children and send them to hell?"

The answer to that form of this question is that I don't believe that God does send His children to hell. As a Baptist, I believe a doctrine called "The Security of the Believer" or "Once Saved, Always Saved." His children – those humans who have made a willful choice to be grafted into His family, through His Son, Jesus – need to fear no condemnation. The question as stated uses a different definition of "His children." It assumes that all humans are children of God.

As an analogy, imagine that you are a parent, and have wonderful children who are obedient and who love you dearly. In time they grow up and go to college, but they come home often, and bring friends whom you treat as if they were your own children. Late one night, a rowdy group of people appears on your front lawn. They are rude, ill-mannered, and obviously intoxicated. They shout for you to let them in, claiming to know your kids from college. You turn to your children and they say that they have never seen these people before.

Would you let them in? Or would you say, "Depart from me, ye workers of iniquity, for I do not know you?" Would you leave them on the lawn? Or call the police, to cast them out into the outer darkness?

So this argument, even if we assume that we can know God's mind, still does not make sense. God's treatment of the lost is rational and just, and God's actions are good.

But there is another problem in this argument: A case can be made that no one winds up in hell who did not ask to go there. As an example, we note in Psalm 139, where the psalmist writes, "If I ascend into the heavens, behold, Thou art there; If I make my bed in hell, behold, Thou art with me." Note that the psalmist refers to making his own bed in hell.

C.S. Lewis – This would be a great time to read his short book, *The Great Divorce* – makes the case that in the end, every man either chooses to accept God's will or chooses to reject it in favor of his own, and at the last, God merely ceases to argue with him.

So the argument fails, yet again.

Doesn't God's foreknowledge make us predestined to fail?

This question is similar to the Problem of Evil, but is slightly different. The idea here is that God created the world knowing that Eve would fall, and that Adam would also sin, thus corrupting the nature of mankind. But if God knew that all of the evil in the world was going to happen as a result of creating mankind, why did he go ahead and do it?

The argument then concludes that either God must lack foreknowledge, or else he simply does not care about human suffering. Or, to phrase it differently, we cannot say that evils are necessary evils if God had the power and foreknowledge to render them unnecessary.

The primary problem with this argument is that we do not know why God created mankind. We have a limited number of facts about God's act of creation, and the rationale is not one of them. We do know from scripture that God's foreknowledge is absolute, and that He "sees the end from the beginning." God's purpose is relevant, because we can only judge the fitness of creation in relation to its purpose.

As an analogy, imagine a mystery writer: In order to write a murder mystery, he must cause one of his characters to be killed. That evil, which he knows from the beginning, is necessary to the work: He cannot write a sincere murder mystery that contains no murder.

By the same token, William Shakespeare could not write Hamlet without killing off Ophelia, Polonius, Hamlet, Gertrude, the King, and Laertes, at the very least – the deaths of each of these is mandated by the style of tragic fiction, which would not permit a fatally flawed character to survive the last act. Gertrude and the King were doomed because they were murderers; Laertes and Hamlet each became Regicides, and Ophelia was driven mad. The nature of the work decreed these deaths.

A writer today can ignore many of these rules, and we can watch the sophisticated cannibal psychologist evade capture in the last act, his heinous crimes not at all atoned, but merely slightly mitigated because he has helped in the capture of some other madman. But such a work is lessened by its refusal to adhere to the rules: It somehow feels like we've been cheated. Had Shakespeare done this, the result would not have been Hamlet.

So the question arises: Could God have simply not created the world, and thereby avoided all of the evil therein? Would this have been better than to have created and then redeemed us? In order to understand how we simply do not know the mind of God, and thus cannot answer, please consider one theory of the rationale of creation (and I cannot stress too much that this is one theory, pieced together from faint fragments and hints, and may be entirely incorrect):

We know that God created angels before creating the earth. We also know that, before the dawn of man, there was war in heaven, and that one third of the angels fell, along with the highest of the archangels, lucifer. In the book of Job, we see a hint of an argument before God, in which God calls satan to account and satan attempts to defend himself through empty excuses.

From this, one might infer (and this is where the theoretical part begins) that mankind was created in order to answer the excuses presented by satan and his angels. We are thus, in that sense, a laboratory experiment, and when the last day arises, we will be used to judge the angels, both holy and unholy. We will be the examples against which they are measured.

For example, it may be put forward as an excuse that some fallen angel was merely following orders. Against that angel, there will stand a human witness, who refused to obey an unjust order. Then God will ask, "Why were you, a spirit who had seen My face, unable to be as faithful as this mere human, who never saw more than My shadow?" – so the theory goes.

In this theory, the evil that befalls humans and the evil that humans do are, in fact, necessary evils. The purpose – a plumb bob to show the failings of the unholy angels – could not be fulfilled, if mankind were not created, had not fallen and been redeemed, or if there were no evil.

But let us go further, and suppose that we do know the mind of God, and that the creation of man and the resulting evil were not necessary – that God by fiat created us, with the intention that some of us should suffer the most horrible of fates. Personally, I believe that to be contrary to the nature of God – I believe that He truly is loving and good – but let us examine the hypothesis.

In addition to the purpose of God, there stands Free Will. It is impossible to say that we act by free will unless it is possible that we might fail; and free will is meaningless unless our failure means something. We must be playing for real stakes, and we must be capable of suffering loss, in order to have free will.

So given that we were created, the choices would be to create us as robotic toys that parrot what we've been told, or to create us as creatures with free will. Here, the comparison between God and a fiction-writer breaks down, because God can imbue His creations with free will, where Shakespeare could not. It probably would not have pleased Shakespeare for his characters to make free will choices. MacBeth would have been a very brief play if the title character had declined to commit regicide.

But even if we ignore free will, and God's unfathomable purposes, would it be unfair to create us? We find an answer in Jeremiah, in the house of the potter. We mentioned this earlier in response to the Problem of Evil. The potter creates two vessels, one as a ceremonial pitcher, to be used in worship, and another to be a crude chamberpot. Does the chamberpot have grounds to complain? Wasn't it the potter's right to make whatever he chose from the clay? Thus, by the right of creation, if God chose to let us experience evil, it is fair and just.

There is, further, the simple fact that we find in Job, that God is God, and we are not. He is the sovereign over all of creation, and if He chooses that bad things happen, who are we to say otherwise? On the surface, this sounds unfair, but that is because we are mentally imagining God as an earthly leader or as one of our peers, and then judging Him accordingly.

God cannot be judged by any man. There is no standard of Justice high enough that we may make a case against Him. There is no law so fundamental as to be binding upon God. But even if there were — we permit earthly leaders to make these sorts of decisions. We permit generals to decide who will live and who will die — who will type letters in a bunker, and who will charge the enemy guns with fixed bayonets. We regard this as normal, when a general achieves his objective through the loss of his men, so why would we charge it as unfair if it is God, instead of a general?

In fact, in order to judge God, we are saying, by implication, that we are more fair than God — that we have a higher understanding of right and wrong, and that we apply that understanding more equitably. I can think of no more ridiculous thing than for a man to believe himself able to judge God.

By the right of His purpose, by the need for Free Will, by His sovereignty, by the fact of His creation, God's actions are fair. We therefore cannot charge Him with being less than benevolent, regardless of what evils befall us. But even if we do, there remains another aspect of this question.

Suppose that there is a man whose life is unfair. He is conceived under the worst of circumstances, born into cruel conditions, lives a life of pain, misery, and abuse, and ultimately dies. Even if we blame God for every evil that has befallen this man, it is within God's power to make right all that has gone wrong. In the book of Job, God restored Job's health and returned to him two-for-one everything that he had lost. So also, in the case of our hypothetical man, God has an eternity to make everything right. This life is but a moment when compared to eternity, and God can literally wipe away every tear from our eyes.

Can we really say, then, in the light of eternity, that it would be better if we had never been created? I do not believe that we can.

Isn't the God hypothesis non-falsifiable, and thus useless?

The idea in this little bit of sophistry is that God's existence does not meet the standards required for the acceptance of a scientific hypothesis, and thus is not worthy of consideration.

There are several problems here, simply in the foundation of this question. First, the question assumes that God's existence is a hypothesis to be tested scientifically. We discussed, much earlier, that science and God are not in conflict, and cannot be in conflict. Secondly, there is the assumption that we should only consider ideas that are "Scientific," and that no other ideas hold any value.

The last point becomes ridiculous when we consider all of the intangibles that are still of value: Love, loyalty, friendship, ethics, logic, imagination, peace, joy, and patience, to name a few. None of these are scientific. One cannot measure "Joy" and quantify it. One cannot make a hypothesis that will explain a person's inner peace. Love is not subject to theories and laws.

To say that a thing can be falsified means that there is at least one test by which we can demonstrate that something is false. For example, application of Newton's laws of motion to the planet Uranus, by Leverrier, in 1846, revealed that Uranus did not follow the predicted path, and thus Newton was falsified. Alan E. Musgrave cites this historical fact in his paper, "Falsification and Its Critics," which he presented to the fourth annual International Congress on the Logic and Methodology of Science, in 1973.

When Neptune was added to the equation, first as a theory and then as an observation, the variance was explained, and the motions complied with the laws. But for a brief moment, Newton was falsified, yet not false. Confused? You should be.

Karl Popper began using Falsification as a substitute for the Scientific method in order to dodge the logical problem of induction versus deduction. We discuss that problem in chapter fourteen, as one of the two arguments that are like atomic bombs. The problem is that Falsification has even larger problems still.

The first is, as we mentioned, that a hypothesis may be falsified without being false, as when Leverrier's observations falsified Newton's laws of motion. It was the laws of motion which were eventually proven correct – well, until they were shown to be false by Einstein's Relativity. There is another problem, known as Duhem's thesis: for every falsification of a hypothesis, there must necessarily exist Auxiliary hypotheses which are accepted without testing them. To discuss it at length here would be an unjustified digression, and quite boring as well.

Does Evolution disprove God?

The short answer is "No, it does not."

The argument underlying this question goes something like this: The Bible says that the world and mankind were created in seven days, and that it happened about 6,000 years ago; Radio-carbon tests, Potassium-Argon tests, and similar data show that the earth is much older than 6,000 years; therefore the Bible is false. In particular, we can see that there existed animals much longer ago than 6,000 years ago, &c., thus they were not all specially created one Friday Afternoon in April, 4004 BC.

Therefore Creation is false, therefore the Bible is false, and therefore we have no Creator.

There are several counter-arguments which have been raised over time, and we'll just touch lightly upon them:

First, there is the **Gap Theory**. In a nutshell, this is the theory that there is a gap in time of an unknown period between Genesis 1:1 and Genesis 1:2. God created the Heavens and the Earth, the gap begins, the dinosaurs rule the earth, there is war in heaven, the dinosaurs all die off, and satan is cast down.

Then, the earth being formless and void, the Spirit moved upon the face of the deep, and the seven days of creation began. This has several points against it: It borders on being an argument from silence, and it contradicts the idea that before the fall of man, all animals were peaceful vegetarians.

Another theory is that the seven days were **not literal days**. The crux of this is that the word "day" can be used to denote eras ("In the days of Moses") or can be used to mean 24 hour periods. In support of this idea, there is the fact that Light, and the sun and moon, by which we mark days and nights, did not exist until after the first day. Against this idea there is the fact that the word used in the original Hebrew is "Yom," which is consistently used in Hebrew to denote a 24-hour period.

Still another theory is an idea called **Omphalos,** which is Latin for "Belly-button." The concept is that Adam and Eve must necessarily have had belly buttons, despite not having been born, and that the world was made with the appearance of age. On the one hand, there is little to recommend this theory, but on the other hand, it is impossible to disprove it. A typical atheist counter-argument is that this makes God into some sort of trickster who is trying to lie to us. This counter-argument is an argument from silence, and assumes that there is no reason for God to have made Dinosaur fossils within the earth, except to trick us. It also casts the atheist into the role of defending God's honor against the charge of "tricksterism."

Still another theory is that the analysis of the **ages and times** denoted by the Bible are incorrect – for example, it was common in Hebrew geneologies to skip generations that were not immediately relevant to the point being made. Note Matthew 1:1, which states, "The Geneology of Jesus Christ, Son of David, Son of Abraham." Since David lived 1000 years before Christ, and Abraham more than 500 years before David, it is clear that generations have been skipped. In fact, over the next few verses, Matthew fills in the gaps by giving us a more fleshed-out geneology.

Within the Ages and Times theory is a nested theory, that God started the earth by Creation, and then permitted it to run without him, and that evolution is merely an instrument of that operation. This viewpoint is sometimes called **Theistic Evolution.**

Another theory is that **dating is in error.** The idea here is that some sort of error has entered the dating methods. For example, the Potassium-Argon method can be called into question if there are high natural levels of Potassium in the surrounding soil. Johansson rejected the Potassium-Argon dating for the skeleton that he named "Lucy," preferring other methods. This argument does suggest that certain constants, such as half-lives or the natural proportions of certain isotopes, may have changed significantly over time.

So which viewpoint is correct on this matter? I can't answer. Several of these theories answer the point, and any of them might be correct. But which ever one chooses to endorse... and it is usually enough, in my experience, to merely demonstrate that because these arguments do exist, the die is not yet cast as far as Creationism is concerned... the basic argument (that evolution "disproves" creation) is false on the face of it. As we have said, since any miracle, including creation, requires a temporary suspension of the laws of nature, those self-same natural laws can not be used to judge a miracle's likelihood.

In addition, we are faced with the problem that Evolution does not answer the most fundamental of questions: How did life start? The honest atheist will say, "We don't know." Some will opine that amino acids formed on their own, formed DNA strands, and those DNA strands developed into the first primitive micro-organisms. Others will posit more fanciful theories, such as panspermia.

Panspermia is the idea that life began on Earth as a result of a "seed" organism – perhaps a bacteria – riding on a meteorite. To date, no meteorite has been shown to have hitch-hiking DNA, but some scientists are convinced that it happened that way. Still others take Panspermia further and posit that we were planted here by some superior race of extraterrestrial beings. Whatever the alleged mechanism, Panspermia doesn't answer the question. At best, it merely moves it back a planet.

A further problem with the Panspermia theory's Extraterrestrial version is that it attempts to distinguish an alien from a god. I once kept an atheist ranting for several days by trying to get him to distinguish panspermia from creation, using as examples Thor, the Norse thunder-god, and Spock, a fictional character from the Star Trek television series. That is to say, if we're going to suppose that a superior being deliberately placed us here, how is that distinct from Special Creation?

In the end, all that we know as a scientific fact is that once there was no life, and now there is. We cannot say, beyond any shadow of doubt, that evolution was the cause; science cannot address whether the laws of science were suspended by a Creation event.

Thus, Evolution whether we consider it "proven" or not in itself, neither proves nor disproves the existence of God.

Isn't God old-fashioned? Isn't church old-fashioned?

I often quote C.S. Lewis. One of my favorite passages in The Screwtape Letters is when Screwtape tells Wormwood that the best way to keep humans from taking an idea seriously is to frame it as "reactionary" or "progressive" or "Old-fashioned" or "modern." Screwtape advised using any adjective except for "true" or "false," to confuse the human.

To apply this: Suppose that God is old-fashioned. Does that mean that He doesn't exist? Certainly not. Isn't belief in God old fashioned? Well, it is old; extremely old, stretching back towards Creation itself. But that does not make it any more, or any less true. God is not subject to our whims and fancies. He does not cease to exist because we find Him unfashionable.

Instead of whether He is old-fashioned, instead ask, "Is He True?"

Didn't man create God?

No one would phrase it quite like that, at least not out loud. The argument – And I'm pretty sure that this is one Screwtape wishes for us not to examine too closely – goes like this:

> **Premise:** Some gods of some religions are false, and even silly.
> **Conclusion:** Therefore all Gods are false and silly.

The unstated premise is that all gods are equally likely, equally true (i.e. false), and should be given the equal amount of weight. This premise is obviously false, rendering the conclusion useless. But it is true that there can exist, at most, exactly one God.

This argument usually takes the form of a pseudo-documentary, detailing the concepts of God known to various peoples. It may claim, for example, that the Hebrew idea of Monotheism actually derives from Egypt's Amarna period, in which Inkhnaton declared that only one god, the sun god Aton, was to be worshipped (In my opinion, it seems more likely that Egyptian Monotheism was a copy of Hebrew Monotheism).

As a general rule, assertions will be made which are based on slight or non-existent evidence, such as a claim that there is no evidence for Hebrew Monotheism before the Exodus – such a claim would be an argument from silence – Or that the Hebrew God was an idea based on Midianite customs (which is not only wrong but moot, since the Midainites were descended from Abraham through his third wife, Keturah).

The question arises: Why would people produce documentaries of this sort and publish them? The answer is simple: Telling someone that what he believes is correct does not sell magazines (or attract advertisers, or sell newspapers).

Are you really so arrogant as to believe that your version of God is true and correct, and all others are false?

We addressed this briefly in the introduction. This argument bases itself upon several bad premises: That to be arrogant is wrong, that to believe is arrogant, and that all religious viewpoints are of equal value.

Let us consider the last point first: It should be readily apparent that not all religious viewpoints are equal. I doubt that anyone would say that the ancient Mayans, who were known for ripping the beating hearts from the chests of their enemies and using their heads as soccer balls, were on the same religious level as, say, the Amish, who practice no violence at all towards man nor beast. And yet that is the implied assumption here. You see that it quickly fails when isolated, unearthed, and examined.

Let us also consider whether belief equals arrogance. Clearly, anyone who believes any one thing also believes that any contrary conclusion is false. If I believe that 2+2=4 (in base 10 integers*) then I must necessarily believe that 2+2 does not equal 5, 17, 38, or 509. Is that arrogance? Or is it merely acknowledgement of the truth? And isn't a man obligated to believe what is true?

Finally, let's define arrogance. What the atheist who makes this argument usually means is not arrogance as pride, but rather confidence in one's conclusion. When you hear him say, "Are you so arrogant…" you should also hear a serpent lisping, "Did God really say…" because within it is a subtle implication – that by believing you are sinning. Belief = arrogance = pride = sin; that is the suggestion, and again, it becomes absurd on the face of it when we unearth it and expose it to the light.

Which version of Christianity is really true?

This question hinges upon the fact that there are about 55,000 different denominations of Christianity. These vary widely. The atheist who asks this question is implying that they cannot all be correct, therefore most of them are wrong (and by further implication, that therefore all of them are wrong, and thus we cannot know Christ – that Christianity, at its core, is necessarily wrong).

The problem here is that 90-95% of all Christians hold 90-95% of the same beliefs. I once held a poll, on an internet bulletin board, asking if posters who were Christians could endorse both the five points of the Gospel as explained by Paul the Apostle, and also endorse the Nicene Creed, a statement of faith that is shared by many denominations. Paul's five points, found in 1 Corinthians 15, are that Jesus Christ died for the sins of mankind, and was buried; that He rose on the third day, and was seen by many; and that He shall return at the Last Day.

An ambiguous word, "catholic," in the Nicene Creed, caused some of the responding posters to state that they could not endorse the Nicene Creed, even though I explained that as used in the creed, "catholic" means "all-encompassing," and not "of or pertaining to the Church of Rome." Despite this, 90% of posters stated that they could endorse both statements, and allowing for the "catholic/Catholic" issue, 95% would have endorsed both. About 80 self-identified Christians responded.

Obviously, this is not a scientific poll. The sample size is very small, and there were no controls against multiple votes. Also, respondents chose whether or not to read the poll, and whether or not to respond. But I believe that this poll supports my assertions concerning the proportions of Christians who believe the same thing. Oh, there are differences – do we sprinkle, dunk, or pour? Shall we use wine or juice? But the differences are minutia, compared with the central questions of Christianity.

C. S. Lewis, in the introduction to Mere Christianity, compares the Christian faith to a large house with a central doorway. To be a member of the household, one must merely live in the house, and which room one chooses to live in – for each room has different rules and different modes of fellowship, suited to those who live therein – is much less important. Lewis believed that we should downplay the differences between denominations in the interest of leading the lost into our common house. From there, which room they choose to live in is between them and the Master of the House.

So, to answer, at last, the question that spurred this discussion: Any denomination that preaches Christ Alone as the one and only path to God and Heaven, and holds to the five points of Paul's gospel, are my brethren.

Which Bible is the right one?

This argument is usually a variant of the prior question, but it has different implications. The Bible was originally written in Hebrew, Aramaic, and Greek. If we wish to go back to the Hebrew and Greek texts, then that is the most perfect edition, and thus the most authoritative.

It is my belief, however, that God does not sleep. I believe that the same Spirit which breathed God's Word into the original writers also breathed into the translators who sought to do their work for the Glory of God. When I pick up the King James Version, written in the common language of 1611, or the New American Standard, in the language of 1970, in either case I am reading the message that God wishes for me to see.

The differences between versions are minutia. The KJV tells us in John 1:5 that darkness cannot "comprehend" the Light; The NASB says that darkness cannot "overcome" the Light. To an atheist, this appears to be a discrepancy. But when we examine the passage – remember the tools we spoke of earlier: Commentaries, Concordances, and References – we discover that the 1611 English word "comprehend" meant "to encompass, to surround, to overcome." We, today, use this word exclusively to refer to the mental process of understanding an idea: When our brain surrounds, encompasses, and overcomes the idea, we say that we "comprehend."

But the fact that the English language has changed does not render the text incorrect. In either case, God expresses the desired idea to us. And by happy coincidence, the darkness can neither comprehend the Light by the 1611 nor the 2011 definitions.

So the answer is: Any version of the Bible which has been faithfully translated from the original texts, with prayer and the guidance of the Holy Spirit, is the "Right Bible."

Doesn't the Bible contain errors and contradictions?

Here we open a can of worms. There are statements in the Bible which appear to contradict themselves, or appear to be inconsistent. It would be easy to be confused by the fact that all of the gospels record a feeding of 5,000, but that Luke also records a feeding of 4,000. The fact that the other three gospels do not mention the feeding of the 4,000, however, does not mean that it did not happen (to believe so would be an argument from silence) but merely means that the others did not mention it.

Each gospel writer wrote for a specific purpose, and followed a specific theme. Events that did not fit the theme were simply not mentioned. The Apostle John goes so far as to tell us, near the end of his gospel, that there is simply not enough room to comprehensively record the entire life of Christ.

Other contradictions arise from problems of translation. The Hebrew language contains about 10,000 distinct words. By contrast, the modern French language contains about 200,000 words (with new words not permitted, by law), and the modern English language contains over 500,000 words. A single Hebrew word can mean "A well-armored warrior" or "one-thousand men" and the distinction is in the context of the passage.

Further, the Bible uses apparent language. The sun rises, the sun sets; in actual fact we know this to be an illusion caused by the rotation of the earth. But if any writer today replaced a phrase such as, "They sat together, holding hands, and watched as the sun sank below the horizon," with "They sat together, holding hands, and watched as the earth rotated such that the sun ceased to be visible, causing the delineation of day and night to cross their longitude," we would consider him a horrible writer. That the earth rotates, causing night and day, is not relevant to the point of the story.

So in considering apparent contradictions, we have to ask what exactly the Bible is trying to tell us. Is it describing the time of day when an event occurred, or are we supposed to understand the movement of heavenly bodies from this passage? Context is everything.

There is also the fact that the Bible writers often assumed that the reader knew what he was talking about. He could thus make a passing reference to Judas buying a field, and the reader was expected to know the full story of what happened to Judas.

We also have to ask if the two contradictory passages are truly contradictory. If I state that something happened in the early evening, and someone else states that the same event occurred in the late afternoon, have we contradicted ourselves, or merely described the same thing in different language?

This leads us to an idea known as "the unexcluded middle." In any given choice of A or B there are four possibilities: A is true, B is true, A and B are true, and neither A nor B is true. As an example, suppose that we are driving on a two-lane highway, with one lane for each direction. We ask ourselves which lane we are in.

If there is no median and no barrier, we may be in the northbound lane, or in the southbound lane, or we may be straddling the yellow line (both lanes) or we may be driving on the shoulder (neither lane). In this situation, there is an unexcluded middle – the answer is not A or B.

So if an atheist poses an apparent contradiction, it is important to ask if it is truly contradictory, or if it is possible that both passages can be read together one consistent story. An example may be found in the death of Judas Iscariot. One gospel explicitly states that Judas returned to the temple, threw the silver on the floor, and that the priests used it to buy a plot of ground wherein to bury strangers and the poor. Judas then hanged himself. Another gospel tells us that Judas bought a field with the money, and fell headlong, bursting open.

While these accounts appear to be contradictory, they actually can both be true. In the latter account, clearly the writer assumed that we already knew the story, and is merely referring to the event in order to confirm his timeline and sequence of events. He therefore did not give us the details that the priests used Judas' money to buy the field (thus, Judas bought the field, albeit through the agency of the priests), nor that Judas hanged himself before falling from the rope and bursting open. A living human body does not usually burst open when it falls, so we must assume that Judas hung in the noose until the rope rotted apart before falling headlong.

The unexcluded middle thus explains the disparity, and reconciles the accounts. I apologize for the graphic nature of that example – there are probably better examples – but the idea of the reconciliation of the accounts should hopefully outweigh any disgust that we may feel.

In answer: No, the Bible does not contradict itself.

How could they make a fire 7 times hotter?

This is another example of an apparent error in the Bible. I actually had this posed to me by a coworker, as proof that the Bible is not factual.

In the book of Daniel, Shadrach, Meshach, and Abednego are to be thrown into a furnace for failing to obey the unjust command of King Nebuchadnezzar of Babylon. The King orders the fire to be kindled seven times hotter than normal. Wood burns at around 500 degrees Fahrenheit (the auto-ignition temperature of paper is 451, as we should remember from reading Bradbury), and seven times as hot would be 3500 degrees, a temperature that the Babylonians would not have had the technology to develop.

There are several problems with this argument. The first is that this period is well within the iron age, and iron is smelted at around 4000 to 5000 degrees Fahrenheit, so the technology did exist to create a fire that seven times hotter than other cooler fires.

Further, there was no scale for the measurement of temperature at that time. Celsius/Centigrade, Fahrenheit, Rankine, and Kelvin scales of temperature have all been developed within the last couple of centuries. The idea of a fire seven times hotter thus cannot be literal and must be metaphorical or hyperbole (or both).

As an example of how it might be hyperbole: if an ancient were ordered to build a fire seven times hotter, and had no comprehension of modern thermodynamics, he might well assume that seven times the fuel meant seven times the temperature. We now would say that seven times the fuel means seven times the heat – which is an entirely different concept – but an ancient would not know this. Thus, in apparent language, one might say that the fire was seven times hotter.

But why seven? Why not five times, or ten times hotter? The ancients often used numbers to express ideas. Seven was the number of completion or perfection. To say that a fire was seven times hotter meant that the fire was completely hot, or perfectly hot... In other words, Nebuchadnezzar called for the hottest possible fire. And this fits precisely with the story.

Isn't Pascal's Wager for Wimps?

Pascal's Wager was a alleged statement by Blaise Pascal, to the effect that if he believed in God and was wrong, the worst case was that he would die and find nothing; Whereas if he did not believe in God, the worst case was that he might die and find himself in Hell. The benefits of believing, which were the hope of Heaven and the avoidance of Hell, outweighed any benefit of not believing.

In arguing that Pascal's wager is a wimpy and cowardly approach to the problem, the atheist is essentially changing the subject. He is painting himself as the brave and defiant human, nobly standing his ground against the Supernatural Creator.

In fact, the picture that we should see here is not a portrait of brave defiance, but rather a petulant child stamping its foot and saying, "I won't, I won't, I won't!" One might as well envision a man in a burning building, when the fireman comes on a ladder to rescue him, saying, "No, that's the coward's way. I'll climb the side of the building and slide down the storm drain."

This is an example of the idea we spoke of earlier, in the question of whether God is Old-fashioned, that the devil would prefer us to use any adjective except "true" or "false" when examining an idea. We should thus examine the question in exactly those terms: Does Pascal's wager yield a true analysis of the facts? And the fact is that it does. So the atheist may call us cowardly, as he shinnies down the drainpipe, but the fact is that to be a Christian is the safer course.

In short – Going to hell is not a brave thing to do, but merely foolish.

Isn't your argument just a God-of-the-Gaps argument?

This argument is typically used as a smokescreen when a Christian makes a good argument. It is usually a straw man (that is, misrepresenting the opponent's argument so that it can be more easily defeated).

A true God-of-the-Gaps argument would take the form: We don't know why X happened, therefore God did it. The idea is that there is a gap in our knowledge and that we Christians are trying to point into that gap and say, "There He is! There's God, in the gap." Of course, we know that God shops for His clothing exclusively in major department stores, so this is simply absurd.*

More often than not, it is the atheist who is seeing God in the gaps, and who has reshaped the argument to fit this mold. I have had atheists accuse me of using a God-of-the-Gaps (GOTG) argument in the argument about Schrodinger's Cat, much later in this book. They love to claim that I am arguing that we do not know why the cat has a dual phase, and that therefore God did it, for example. That is not the argument at all. The argument there is that the cat has a dual phase, we know that it has a dual phase, and that a dual phase is impossible in an objective universe.

An atheist will seize any opportunity to claim that an argument is GOTG, and the fact that the argument says no such thing will not phase him. The only reply possible is to say, "No, you're creating a straw man; read my argument again."

Why hasn't God made more of an effort to make Himself obvious to me?

The atheist here wants to have his cake and eat it too. He places the burden of proof onto God, and then waits for God to do the heavy lifting. At the same time, he dismisses any casual evidence of God, including the testimony of friends, because that would require that he actually seek God, instead of merely waiting for Him.

God does sometimes reveal Himself to people in powerful ways. Paul's Damascus Road conversion stands as an example. But God does not always use that method. One might opine that He uses the most effective method for each person.

One should also recall Jesus' response to the Rich Man in the parable: "Even if One were to rise from the dead, still they would not believe." So the answer to the question is that the atheist can not see the presence of God because he's not looking for it. One would also do well to recall the Apostle Paul's assertion, in the first Chapter of Romans, that God has revealed Himself to us through Creation itself. If Paul is correct, then the fault lies not with God, but with the atheist.

We cannot know, on this side of eternity, how many times God has attempted to make Himself known to us, only to be ignored and dismissed. Earlier, I described an event in which I believe that God spoke to me through a radio broadcast, a printed magazine, and the words of a friend, each of which recited a certain scripture verse that applied very well to my circumstances. But I was willing to dismiss the radio and the quarterly as coincidence, until the man spoke those very words again.

When we are told that "God has never spoken to me," we should ask, "Have you been listening?"

Isn't God Unscientific?

God need not be scientific. But the implied argument goes like this: There is no scientific proof for God's existence, therefore one cannot be "scientific" and still believe in God. This is an example of something called a "False dichotomy." A false dichotomy exists when we examine only two of many possible answers. When we talked about whether the Bible contradicts itself, we discussed an idea called the unexcluded middle. That applies here. The atheist would like us to believe that either one is a man of science, or else one is a man of faith, but not both (though certainly one might be neither).

In fact, since the idea behind Divine Intervention is that God stands outside of our universe, and can suspend its laws at will, there is no conflict between science – which deals exclusively with the laws of nature – and faith, which deal exclusively with those things beyond the natural. One can certainly be a Christian and a Scientist.

Jesus Christ was not "The Best and Wisest of men" because He once cursed a fig tree.

This argument was put forward by a prominent nineteenth century mathematician, as part of his justification for not belonging to the Christian faith. The fact that Jesus became angry, he argues, and cursed the fig tree for refusing to bear fruit for Him, demonstrates that He was unfair, and thus did not show Godly attributes, and therefore was not God. Formalizing the logic:

P1: If Jesus was God, then He was the best and wisest of men;
P2: Jesus was not the best and wisest of men
C: therefore Jesus was not God.

The first premise is suspect, in and of itself. "Best and Wisest" leaves a lot of room for ambiguity. But the second premise is the weakest. It stands upon a syllogism something like this one:

P1: If Jesus was the best and wisest, He would always be fair.
P2: Cursing the fig tree was unfair.
C: Therefore Jesus was not the best and wisest of men.

Premise 1 is fatally flawed. There is no standard of fairness that can be applied to God. As we discussed earlier, God is sovereign, and can do as He pleases with creation; God is the creator, and has the right to follow His design with Creation; and God has the ability, and all of eternity, to make right anything which seems to us to be unfair in this lifetime.

The second premise is also flawed, for the same reason: If Jesus is the Sovereign Creator God, then He has the right to do as he pleases with creation, and the fairness of the action is irrelevant. For Jesus to do something which strikes us as unfair – and unfair to whom, by the way? To the fig tree? – does not make him unfair, immoral, or unwise.

In fact, that Jesus had human emotions – anger, sorrow, joy, pain – demonstrates the completeness of His humanity. He was just like us, but lived sinlessly; He knows our pain by experience. He was fully human, and also fully God.

So the "best and wisest" argument is simply absurd.

I pointed this out to an atheist once – he was daring me to refute the book in question – and his response was that the mathematician was joking, and was merely demonstrating the absurdity of Christianity. A typical atheist response: When the argument collapses, pretend that it wasn't a real argument and that they didn't really mean it.

Iron Chariots? Seriously?

A passage in Kings describes the armies of the Israelites as being universally victorious when fighting in the hill country, because God was with them, but states that they could not prevail upon the plains, for the people there had iron chariots. This seems to imply that God was not omnipotent, in that He could not overcome Iron Chariots.

This is an example of the sorts of arguments posed as contradictions or errors in the Bible. Earlier, we talked about Bible help-materials, and one that is very useful here is the Matthew Henry Commentary.

Matthew Henry was a Presbyterian Minister who lived in eighteenth century England. He was given a great insight into the Bible, and his life's work was the creation of a commentary that explains and clarifies many obscure passages. In reference to this passage, he points out that it is not that the Israelites could not overcome iron chariots, but that they feared to try. Thus the failing belongs not to God, but to men who lacked faith in Him.

When you are faced with a difficult passage of this sort, I strongly recommend finding the passage in Matthew Henry, and reading his wisdom.

So, which god is God, anyway?

This argument is intended to suggest that even if a person clears the apparently insurmountable hurdle of proving that God exists, he must then demonstrate that the God who exists is the YHWH of the Bible, and lacking that, should not accept the existence of God. The conclusion is, of course, absurd.

We cleared the insurmountable hurdle of probing God's existence in the interim between chapters 1 and 2, with the two arguments that are like atomic bombs. In the second argument, we demonstrated that there must necessarily exist an Omniscient Superobserver, and that the Omniscient Superobserver meets the criteria to be called a god.

So which god is God?

As we look for a place to begin, there are some axioms that seem readily apparent to me:

Axiom 1: Whichever God is the true God will have been worshipped from prehistory until today.

This necessarily excludes all of the Norse gods, for example, as well as the Greco-Roman and Egyptian gods, and the Canaanite/ Punic gods, all of whom have faded from their former renown. This also eliminates any Johnny-come-lately gods that may have cropped up in the last couple of thousand years. Even the monotheistic Aton worship is excluded.

Axiom 2: The True God is a Personal God.

By this, we mean that he has a personality and can interact one on one with humans, as a man interacts with another man. This excludes the pantheistic concepts of God as One-ness with the universe. We noted earlier that the Omniscient Superobserver required by Berkeley's Treatise must be personal because He observes our individuality and personality. We are thus made in His image.

We are essentially left with YHWH or Allah as the one true God. Each of the modern montheistic religions – Judaism, Christianity, and Islam – claims an unbroken chain of worship for its God, beginning with the first man and extending to the present day.

These religions are, to a certain extent, mutually contradictory. That is to say, If Judaism is correct, then Islam is wrong; and if Islam is correct, Christianity is wrong. There is even some discord between Christianity and Judaism, but it hinges upon a single point of belief, which we will discuss later. Since Judaism and Christianity observe the same God, we can skip the distinction for the moment.

The excluded middle is established by certain passages from each religion. For example, Isaiah tells us that there is exactly one God. From the 40th chapter onward, there are repeated declarations of God's unity, distinctness, and unique nature. Even the name by which God declares Himself to Moses, YHWH ("I Am") distinguishes Him by His existence. In John 14:6, Jesus tells us that He is the Way, the Truth, and the Life; no man comes to the Father except through Him.

In Islam, however, Jesus is considered a prophet. In Christianity, neither Mohammed nor Allah are given this sort of respect. This disparity means that we cannot weld these two religions together and say that they both have some truth to them, or some similar wishy-washy pronouncement. If Islam is true, then Christianity is wrong about the role of Jesus Christ, and if Christianity is true, then Islam is completely wrong.

But it does not stop there. As C. S. Lewis pointed out in *Mere Christianity,* Jesus cannot be "just a prophet" or a good man who said nice things. Jesus went around claiming to be God. When a man claims to be God, one of three things must be true: Either he is lying, or he is insane, or He truly is God. But he cannot be "A good man" or "A good prophet." These roles are excluded: A good man or a good prophet does not make insane claims about himself, and does not tell cruel lies that will cause someone to invest their lives in a deception. It is a logical assessment to believe that Jesus was insane, or the cruelest of liars, or that He was God.**

But a prophet? No, that is not possible.

So Islam is impossible. It cannot be the True Religion, because it commits a logical absurdity in its placement of Jesus Christ. We are left with Judaism and Christianity.

Christianity considers itself the completion of Judaism and the fulfillment of its teachings. For example, on the one hand we are given the sacrificial system for the remission of sins, including blood sacrifice, but on the other hand we are told (in Psalm 51, for example) that such sacrifices are meaningless to God, and that He instead desires our hearts and our obedience.

These dual themes continue throughout the Tanakh, and seem to offer a puzzle. Jesus himself remarked on this, by citing Psalm 110:1 and then asking the religious leaders how the coming Messiah could be both David's son and David's Lord.

With complete hindsight, we now see the reconciliation of the two themes; The Messiah is a conquering King and a suffering Servant at the same time. In Romans, Paul reconciles the legal aspects of this dual theme. In Hebrews, we see that Jesus is the ultimate High Priest, who carries Himself as the Sacrifice into the Temple to Himself and thus fulfills all three roles, as Priest and God and Sacrifice.

Ultimately, then, Christianity fulfills Judaism.

Now, the astute reader will say, "Wait a moment. There are other religions that claim to be the fulfillment or the restoration of Christianity. How is the claim of Christianity towards Judaism different from these claims?"

The answer is that Christianity accepts the Jewish scriptures as written, and still claims to fulfill their prophecies. Other religions claim to have the true or correct version of Christian Scriptures, and claim to fulfill these "revised" scriptures. These must argue that Christians got it all wrong, and that they alone can set it right. Christians, on the other hand, believe that the Jewish scriptures got it right, and just need the fulfillment of their prophecies.

This is an important distinction.

So where does that leave us? Well, we quickly winnowed the field down to the three monotheistic religions, and we can clearly see that of these, Christianity is the best path. It does not make sense to take another path.

So which god is God? Jesus Christ, who has come in the flesh, and who is the LORD of all. He is God.

How can one being, however transcendent, demand that another being worship Him?

The Atheist who first posed this question to me argued that no being has a right to demand worship from another being. I discussed the conversation earlier in this book, while we were discussing the use of Bible Help Materials such as concordances, along with the etymology of the word "Worship," so I won't bore you with an unnecessary repetition.

The main points to remember are that, first of all, the premise is absurd, and second, worship is the only natural reaction to the presence of God. We who have lived under the Constitution of the United States are tempted to believe that because all men are created equal, that therefore all creatures are equal. We, who refuse to have titled Lords and Dukes and hereditary Peers, are tempted to believe that being created equal – that is, equal in value and equal before the law – also makes us equal in nature.

To be equal in value and equal before the law does not mean identical, nor that we should all hold the same station. Some men are better at being plumbers than being professors. Some men are better at being surgeons than being bus drivers. We appoint (we hope) the best and brightest to be judges. To these we give a measure of respect: We call them by an honorific name, and we heed their words closely. We take pains to avoid offering them disrespect or contempt.

One might easily say that we fear a judge in the sense, if not the magnitude, that we fear God.

But that's not the same, you say. We still hold judges accountable. When a judge takes off the black robe, he is again a mere mortal, and gone are the honorific titles and the courtly respect. The respect we afford a judge is a mere shadow of the respect that Christians show to their God.

Well, that's true. But the reason that the respect we afford a judge is a pale shadow of the worship of God is that a judge is a pale shadow of God himself. Where a judge calls us to account for the laws of man, God calls us to account for crimes against each other and against the universe. Where a judge grants us a limited clemency, God offers us unlimited Grace. If the scale of respect is different, the scale of the one respected is different.

So it is absurd to say that one being cannot demand respect from another, or even service; we see it among our own species. How much more then might we call out, one to another, declarations of the Worth-ship-full nature of God Almighty, who is transcendent and holy?

Wasn't the Catholic Church mean to Galileo?

Here, history becomes schizophrenic. We have been taught that Galileo got a bad shake, and that he was persecuted for believing in a heliocentric solar system. History, however – real history that is; the documents and details – tells another story.

Galileo Galilei, known to history by his given name, probably did not get his just deserts. He did live his last years under house arrest, and was forbidden to publish without permission, but within his house he was permitted to write and to experiment to his heart's content. He wrote his best works while under house arrest.

Galileo had already revolutionized physics by demonstrating Aristotle to be wrong, and had explained the parabolic trajectory of cannonballs and the relationship between weight and gravitational acceleration. He had revolutionized astronomy by discovering mountains on the moon and phases of Venus, along with moons around Jupiter. He used the latter discovery to champion his support for Copernicus' theories of heliocentricity.

But Galileo was abrasive as a person, and his outspoken antipathy towards Jesuits probably led to the 1616 proscription of heliocentricity. Galileo was still a free man at this point. He could easily have traveled anywhere in Europe and lived well, publishing any idea that popped into his head, heliocentric or otherwise. But in 1623, fortune appeared to favor Galileo: His friend was elected Pope Urban VIII. Galileo believed that he had protector in the new pope, and allowed himself to publish again.

He wrote a paper savagely dissecting an anonymous paper written by a Jesuit, concerning the nature of comets. Galileo was ruthless, hiding behind his highly-placed patron. What he did not realize was that the anonymous Jesuit writer was his friend, Urban VIII. This strained the relationship between them.

When Galileo published his book, *Dialogue on the Two Chief World Systems*, in 1630, he presented both the Ptolemaic and the Copernican systems, so as to circumvent the 1616 prohibition on publishing Copernican theory. The church initially allowed it to be published, but in 1633, when it became obvious that Galileo had used a loophole to publish Copernican theory, further publication was prohibited and Galileo was tried before a religious court. One should note that Galileo could have avoided this fate by self-exile, but he remained in Italy by choice.

His punishment for defying the authorities was that he had to stay home and work on what eventually became his greatest work, Two New Sciences, which was published in 1638.

And all of this could have been avoided, had he been able to avoid calling the Pope an idiot.

Was Galileo treated unfairly? Well, in our society today, lawyers would be lining up to offer writs of habeas corpus on Galileo's behalf, but like most seventeenth century Europeans, Galileo did not have the benefit of our Constitution.

But let's grant the assumption that Pope Urban VIII was cruel to Galileo. For a single Christian, or even a group of Christians, to perform an act that is contrary to Christian morals does not prove Christian morals to be flawed. It only proves that the Christians in question did not adhere to their principles.

To put this in different terms: If an Australian robs a bank, does this prove that all Australians are bank robbers? Of course not. Does it disprove the existence of Australia? Certainly not. So why would we assume that how Urban VIII got along with Galileo has any bearing on whether or not Jesus Christ was the Son of God?

This argument has a variant, which is the implication that the Spanish Inquisition somehow proves something about Christianity. A few minutes of research into the causes and nature of the Spanish Inquisition will dispose of that argument as well, or one can simply point out the irrelevance of the behavior of individuals.

If you had not been raised as a Christian, you wouldn't be one now.

This argument bases itself upon statistics which suggest that a very high percentage of people, worldwide, die as adherents of the religion of their parents. The underlying argument is that you, as a Christian, are only a Christian because you are culturally biased towards Christianity.

The first objection is that the statistics do not exclude those persons who are never exposed to any religion other than their own. The second problem is that the statistics do not distinguish the various religions of the world. If they did, we might learn, for example, that 99% of persons born in Christian cultures die Christians, whereas only 70% of Buddhists died as Buddhists, or that only 50% of Hindus died as Hindus. These statistics would be highly suggestive, and would destroy the stated argument, without contradicting the stated statistic.

But even if we accept the stated statistic as being valid and meaningful, which it is clearly not, the fact that some people do convert to other religions demonstrates that cultural bias cannot possibly be the only factor in the acceptance or rejection of a religion. Further, if we assume that one of the world religions is factually correct, it follows that a high number of people worldwide will be born into a culture which accepts the true religion. We cannot logically expect people to reject a religion that they discover to be factually true, just because it is the preferred religion of the culture into which they were born.

Thus, the fact that a person who has been born into a culture accepts the tenets of that culture does not mean that the tenets of that culture are therefore wrong.

This argument thus is based upon a meaningless statistic and an illogical conclusion drawn from that statistic.

What about Cognitive Biases?

Cognitive biases are basically another way of saying "Fallacies." A bias is an angled cut or a slope. In logic and reasoning, a bias carries the idea that two dissimilar things are being compared as if they were similar. In the case of a cognitive bias, we are asked to assume that some people reason fallaciously because they are unable to see that the things that they are comparing are dissimilar.

The argument immediately prior to this one assumes a cognitive bias towards the religion of one's culture. Another example of cognitive bias can be seen on Mount Rushmore. At the time that Mount Rushmore was sculpted, Theodore Roosevelt was seen in the same light as Washington, Lincoln, and Jefferson; thus his face is seen on Mount Rushmore. History is a bit more reserved towards Theodore today; While a notable and effective president, few people in our generation would class him with the first, third, and sixteenth presidents. The cognitive bias in his case is that one tends to place greater importance on more recent events; while his memory was fresh, he was more highly honored.

But even if we were to accept the atheists' arguments that we are more responsive to Christianity because of cognitive biases, that would not imply that Christianity is therefore false.

To illustrate this: If we assume that one of the world religions is true, and if we further assume that equal proportions of persons are cognitively biased towards each world religion, then we can clearly see that cognitive bias in itself does not speak to the objective truth or falsity of the religion towards which one is biased. Some people would be cognitively biased towards the true religion, and others against it. The bias and the truth are unrelated.

The key to understanding this argument is the word "Bias." We have become culturally biased against biases, because we subconsciously associate the word "bias" with racial bias. The atheist is trying to use the word "bias" to make you retract your argument by making you react to the word "bias." Your response needs to ignore the cultural significance of the word "bias" and to address the facts of the argument.

If someone were to say, "You say that because you have cognitive biases," a good response would be, "So what?" as would, "And so do you." One is reminded of the passage from the C. S. Lewis book, *A Pilgrim's Regress*. A student of rhetoric is instructed to answer the argument that two plus two equals four by answering, "You say that because you are a mathematician." In this case, as in that one, the point is to ignore the truth or falsity of your argument by arguing about the nature of the your argument.

Bring the point back to "True" or "False."

What about Russell's Teapot?

The argument, whenever an Atheist brings up Russell's teapot, is inevitably along the line: "You can no more prove the existence of your God than I can prove that there is not a celestial teapot orbiting Jupiter." This is a summary of a longer argument by Bertrand Russell.

The problem with this argument is that it implies that we cannot seriously assert God's existence until we can objectively demonstrate his existence under laboratory conditions. When you see this argument, first make note of the fact that the Atheist is posing an argument based upon a facetious point (the "Teapot"). The argument is going to become strange. Be prepared.

You might want to raise the Schrodinger/Berkeley argument (from chapter fourteen) at this point. If you don't have time (or patience) for the entire thing, you can always simply bring in Berkeley. If the Atheist agrees that a sound is a perception, and not an objective thing, then you can progress through Berkeley's assertion that the universe is thus non-objective and into the conclusion that in a non-objective universe, God must exist; Having proven God's existence, the teapot becomes irrelevant.

On the other hand, if the Atheist insists that the universe is objective, and that the vibrations in the air exist regardless whether or not we perceive them as sound, then the Atheist cannot reasonably argue that God is only as logical as a teapot orbiting Jupiter. After all, the Atheist obviously believes in imperceptible sound waves, the existence of which can never be proven; It is therefore not ridiculous to believe in a God whom you cannot see.

So at worst, Berkeley deflates the argument; at best, He permits you to prove God, rendering the argument moot.

---

* The reader is asked to excuse my strange sense of humor.

** John McDowell expands this concept from C. S. Lewis "Poached Egg" argument into what he calls the "Lunatic, Liar or Lord" Trilemma, in his book, *More than a Carpenter*, *q.v.* One may find the roots of the argument, though not explicitly spelled out, in G. K. Chesterton's *The Everlasting Man*, *quo vide*.

CHAPTER SEVEN

Atheistic Absurdities

When Argument Becomes Ridicule

ATHEISTS, BLESS THEIR pointed little heads, love to make arguments that not even they take seriously. The advantage (to their eyes) of a facetious argument is that if they are refuted, they can always say, "Well, I was just joking!" and if they are not, then the whimsical nature of the argument will make them seem witty – or so they hope. One such argument was mentioned earlier: The "Can God make a rock so big" question. We have given that one all the attention that it deserves – it is a logically improper question, assuming two contradictory things.

Another such argument is called "Last-Thursdayism" and is sometimes raised as a Reduction-to-Absurdity (Reductio Ad Absurdum if you like arguing in Latin) for the Christian argument of Omphalos.

Omphalos is Latin for Bellybutton. We mentioned it earlier. One explanation for why a strict and literal interpretation of the Bible places Creation about 6000 years ago, but some earthly objects (fossils, for example) appear older, is that the earth was created with the appearance of age. That is, at the moment of creation, God made fossils and set rocks that had certain proportions of chemicals (Potassium and argon, for example) so that it would appear that the world was quite a bit older. The author of this theory is Henry Gosse.

The argument is called Omphalos because it holds that Adam and Eve must have had bellybuttons – they would have been created looking precisely like their offspring, all of whom would have this same scar. There is no true counter-argument, since no possible evidence can refute this argument. And while the argument itself is rather rigid – a person who chooses to endorse this argument chooses to be very dogmatic on the age of the earth and the literalness of the timeline – the fact that such an argument exists is proof that the age of the earth is not a settled matter. One may choose to believe one age or another, but no one can say that there is no other possible answer.

Counters to this argument are generally in one of two veins: One may ask why God would make the earth with the appearance of age – I've actually had atheists become defensive of God's character, claiming that he is not a trickster, intent on deceiving mankind, for example, which is a very strange situation indeed – or one may invoke a reduction-to-absurdity, such as "Last Thursdayism."

The idea of Last Thursdayism is that the universe was destroyed last Wednesday, but was re-created exactly the way it had been, the next day (Last Thursday), complete with the memories in your head. Thus you are unaware of the destruction of the universe or its re-creation. The atheist then challenges you to refute the idea; and if you cannot, he will assert that it is just as sensible as Omphalos, and therefore Omphalos is also a silly and useless idea.

This is, of course, illogical. First, it is not a true Reduction-to-absurdity, because it does not follow the implications of your idea in order to reach the clearly silly position, but rather makes up another silly position and then equates it to Omphalos. As such, it is a reduction-to-absurdity of a straw man.

It does, however, make one valid point: There is nothing to support Omphalos aside from the assertion that it is possible. For this reason, I would strongly caution anyone not to dogmatically assert Omphalos, but merely to raise it as an alternative theory—that is, as proof that at least one other theory fits all of the known facts. It should not be a dogma, but an antidote to dogmatic atheism.

Another absurdity that atheists like to raise is the Flying Spaghetti Monster, also called Pastafarianism. Pastafarianism is another Straw-Man/Reduction-To-Absurdity combination, and if we were to state its logical backbone syllogistically, it would look something like this:

P1: Pastafarianism is just like a religion
P2: Pastafarianism is silly
C: Therefore all religions are silly.

It is true, beyond contest, that some religions and some beliefs are silly. As a general example, the John Frum Cargo Cults are rather silly at the first blush, although one can understand how the cultists might come to believe such things, given their observations and the inferences that they made from them.

But it is a huge leap from "Some religions are silly" to "All religions are silly." The problem lies in the first premise.

Pastafarianism is not "Just like a religion." Pastafarianism is a satire of religion. The difference is that no one truly believes it, and its adherents describe their faith tongue-in-cheek, all the while winking at the camera.

In the last chapter, there was also an Atheistic absurdity known as Russell's teapot. This follows the same pattern as Pastafarianism: Russell's Teapot is absurd; God (in the Atheist's opinion) is like Russell's Teapot; therefore God is (in the Atheist's opinion), also absurd. As we discussed earlier, Berkeley is an excellent tool to deflate it.

If you should encounter a Pastafarian or a Last-Thursdayist, the best recourse is to simply try to point out the errors of their logic, and then to try to get the discussion back on track. But if they insist of taking the tack that their argument is no less silly than yours, it is time to thank them for their time, and then to shake the dust off of your sandals as you leave.

Remember what we said much earlier on: A sincere seeker of truth will not mock you, and will carefully consider your words. Someone whose goal is to back you into a corner and yell "Gotcha!" is not seeking truth, but an argument.

BETWEEN CHAPTERS;

A Brief Moment to Rest Your Mind

BY THIS POINT, you may have "Idea Soup" in your head. You're probably starting to wonder how you can possibly hold all of these thoughts and ideas in your head at the same time, and still have any mental faculties left with which to tackle an atheist's arguments. Don't panic. And don't worry. The answer is simpler than you think.

"Be not conformed to this world, but be ye transformed, by the renewing of your minds." –Romans 12:2

The psalmists used to insert pauses into their songs. You'll see the word "Selah" in many of the psalms. It's there as a musical interlude, or as a pause for contemplation and reflection. Apply this in internet discussions: When some atheist poses some seemingly powerful argument, or really throws you a curve ball, you are not required to immediately pound out a response on the keyboard. You can simply wait and respond the following morning. If the atheist presses you for prompt response – which is probably quite unfair, given that nine out of ten atheist arguments are cut and pasted from some other website – it is perfectly acceptable to say, "Let me think about it, and I'll respond when my mind is fresh."

There is no shame in pausing to let an idea stew in your brain. You can step back, have a glass of water, look up relevant verses, check your Bible help materials (concordances, commentaries, and Bible dictionaries), and even sleep on the idea overnight. Your most powerful tool, however, is prayer. Pray that God will open your eyes to see the solution. Pray that He will give you words to write, and that He will be glorified in the resulting discussion.

I have often found that a formidable argument, from a seemingly undefeatable opponent, will simply unravel if I come back to it after a night's sleep and a session of prayer.

Relax. Renew your mind. Use the helps and tools available to you. Speak to the Logos Himself to find the logic of the problem. And return to the question when you are rested and have been able to consider the issue carefully.

Selah.

CHAPTER EIGHT

The Meaning of Life

I KNOW WHAT you're thinking: I can't possibly intend to explain the Meaning of Life in a little paperback book designed for Cavemen, can I? Well, yes, I intend to do precisely that. Don't worry, it'll be painless. We discussed in the introduction that the specialized words of Philosophy and Theology are merely small ideas putting on airs. Now we will demonstrate that the Holy Grail of modern Philosophy, the Meaning of Life, is much simpler than you might think... And for an encore I'll tell you where to find the real Holy Grail.

First of all, what do we mean by the Meaning of Life? It's a glib little phrase, and rolls nicely off of the tongue, but it symbolizes the efforts and life's-work of many men. Now, a few of you reading this will smirk, knowing that you've already found the Meaning of Life. The rest of us, however, are going to take it in steps.

When we say, "Meaning of Life" we really mean, "How will it make the slightest difference in the big picture that I was here, now, doing this?" And we're certainly not the first to contemplate this thought. I'd like to draw your attention to the Book of Ecclesiastes, in the Bible. It was written by Solomon, somewhere around 1000 BC.

In a Bible Survey class one evening, the minister leading the group remarked that the Book of Ecclesiastes consists of Solomon looking back over his life and saying, "What a fool I have been!" One of the students quipped, "When a man's been married 300 times, that's easy to say."

But the minister was right: Ecclesiastes is a survey of possible meanings in life, and a brief examination of why each of them is not the true Meaning of Life. The phrases that keep popping up are "Vanity of vanities" and "Striving after the wind."

Solomon catalogs many things that are futile pursuits – Labor for labor's sake, and achievement for achievement's sake; the study of History; the pursuit of wisdom; Pleasure; Wine; Ornamental Horticulture; Landscaping; Accumulation of wealth; Patronage of the arts; and the honors of greatness are among those he mentions in the first two chapters alone. It is noteworthy that Solomon is likely to be the only philosopher who declares the pursuit of wisdom to be foolishness (see Ecc. 1:17-18).

The book of Ecclesiastes is clearly written as an intellectual struggle. One senses on the one hand that Solomon is trying to find a core nugget of wisdom in which to anchor his spirit, and yet even wisdom itself seems futile to him; When he has gathered all the wisdom in the world, what will he do with it? Even if he is wise in all that he does, his work and wisdom can be undone by a foolish son; If he does great feats of labor, they can be undone if his successor does not share his vision. In the end, in the last two verses, we see him cornered by an inescapable conclusion.

An interesting parallel reading can be found in the writings of Lev Tolstoy, the 19th century Russian Nihilist who gave us *War and Peace* and *Anna Karenina*. Those two books may or may not be the best novels ever written, but are certainly among the longest and most complex. I would turn your attention, however, to one of the Count's smaller works, *Confession*. In it, he details the inner struggles that plagued him as he tried to resolve the reason for his existence.*

He quotes extensively from Ecclesiastes, and draws parallels with his own inner conflicts. King Solomon and Count Tolstoy both tried to find peace through pleasure, but found it vain; through public works, but found it striving after the wind; through family and through power and through labor and through every enterprise of which men are capable, but found them all empty.

Tolstoy had already written the great works that made him famous, and he was acknowledged as a man of letters throughout the world. He was of the nobility, and held great power over his serfs; He had a family, and children, and sufficient wealth to free him from any material want. All of the good things that we consider the blessings of fortune were in his hand, and still, like Solomon, he was not satisfied.

Solomon expresses his conclusion as an epiphany, without drawing the steps between his starting place and his conclusion. He tells the young to simply follow God. Tolstoy is more precise and more open in his steps. He talks of his insomnia, and of suicidal thoughts – he states that he hid his ropes and his guns, lest he end his own life for want of meaning. But in the end, he struck upon a solution: There is one bridge between the finite and the infinite, and that is the Church.

In this phrase, Tolstoy is not just saying, "The church is the only place where they talk about spiritual stuff, so this must be true." He is saying that because we go looking for the Meaning of Life and the connections between the tangible and the intangible, that we are obviously made for more than eating, drinking, and making merry. There is an intangible world, or else why would we know to seek one?

And the only connection between the intangible things and this physical world is in the Church. Only the Church can bridge the mysteries between the physical life that sustains the body and the spiritual life that sustains the soul. C. S. Lewis, in *A Pilgrim's Regress*, speaks of finally reaching the point of "throwing himself into the arms of Old Mother Kirk" (which is, metaphorically, taking a leap of faith into the Church – Kirk comes from the same Frisian root-word which gives us "church"). Lewis had this same sort of ultimate conclusion: Where reason and fortune and fame cannot take us, the Church bears us gladly.

In contrast to these wise men who found the answer, consider Franz Kafka, the Czech philosopher and writer whose very name has become a synonym for futility. Kafka also tried to find purpose, but the core of his philosophy excluded God. He examined the noble purposes in which men invest their lives, such as supporting their families, or pursuing justice. One of his writings concerns the building of the great wall of China, for example, and another concerns a man who begs for the mercy of a coal merchant, but who would have had as much success if he had tried to fly on his coal-shovel.

Kafka could not see that life would be that much the worse – and in fact might have been better – if he had awakened one morning to find that he had become an enormous cockroach. We know this because he wrote a story exploring that idea. Kafka's every word was heavy, dark, and gloomy, leaving the reader depressed and saddened. Clearly, Kafka could find no meaning worthy of being invested with his life, and Kafka ultimately ended it.

Why, we ask, is it so tragic, so unbearable, to live a life that has no meaning? Why did Kafka, Tolstoy, and all those folks make such a big deal about it? Clearly, there is something within us that seeks a greater purpose. A human soul and a human life is too magnificent and too wondrous a thing to invest in vain and meaningless pursuits. We desire something more; we are shaped for something greater. There is a place within us that desires to be filled. Some have called it a "God-shaped vacuum," (a quote that is often attributed to either Augustine or Blaise Pascal**, and occasionally to Jean Calvin) or have said that He has set eternity in our hearts (Ecc. 3:11).

This is why men strive to know the meaning of life. Those who begin by excluding God, or by considering Him "an unlikely theory" or an "unhelpful hypothesis" are doomed to fail in their quest for meaning. Those who scorn God as a bogeyman or a fairy-tale, and who compare him to magic unicorns or flying spaghetti monsters will never find the meaning that they seek.

That is not to say that one cannot be happy without God; many have managed to immerse themselves in empty pleasures, and some have even taken joy in the emptiness of their shallow lives. But any man who feels the emptiness of the vacuum within, and tries to fill it with anything other than God, must necessarily fail.

The meaning of life is nothing that we can impose from within. Albert Camus attempted to support this idea, in works such as *L'Etranger,* but could not defend it and finally abandoned the idea. We cannot make our lives be meaningful. We can invest our lives in things that have meaning to us – good causes, good deeds, family, friends, and a thousand other ends – but we cannot make our lives meaningful without God.

Tolstoy tried that as well. When he was at his most suicidal, seeking a reason not to hang himself, he had already written, published, and been recognized for his great works. He was titled, was wealthy, had a family whom he loved, and was well-regarded in his community by both his peers and the peasants who tended his lands. Yet all of these potential meanings from within – recognition, wealth, reproduction, family, acclaim – were not enough to fill his needs.

The Meaning of Life is the service of God – He alone gives our lives meaning, and without Him, we are striving after the wind. Solomon, Tolstoy, and Lewis agree, and even Kafka would admit that no other purpose or meaning comes close to meeting the requirements. Serve God, and Him alone.

There it is for your reading pleasure: the Holy Grail of Philosophy: The Meaning of Life. You knew it all along, I'll bet. You, also, have eternity written on your heart.

But I promised you the true Holy Grail, as well.

Consider the Holy Grail legends: It is the cup in which Joseph of Arimathea caught the blood of Christ; it was the cup used at the Last Supper; it sustains the faithful despite any hardship or struggle; it appears to those who seek it; It is for the pure of heart; and those who drink from it have eternal life.

Now think for a moment of similar cups. Is there a cup said to contain – either truly, or as a metaphor, or somewhere in between – the blood of Christ? Is there a cup which confers upon the drinker – or if you prefer, which is only drunk by those who have obtained – Eternal Life?

What cup, before we drink from it, requires of us that we examine and purify our hearts? What cup, drunk from by our Lord at the Passover, sustains the weak and weary?

Ah, you've guessed my riddle. Yes, friends: The Holy Grail will be served to the Pure of Heart (or at least those temporarily Pure of Heart) this very Sunday, in a great many Christian houses of worship.

There is more to the cup; the Grail; the communion of the Saints. When a young Jewish man sees a young Jewish woman whom he desires to wed, he asks his parents to approach her family. The parents of the bride and groom work out the details—dowry and so forth – and only then do the bride and groom meet. As a proposal, the groom pours a cup of wine; if the bride drinks it, they are engaged.

The groom will go away for a time, and return unexpectedly to claim his bride and fulfill the marriage contract. Christ used marriage as an analogy for the relationship between God and mankind: The Church is called the Bride of Christ, and Salvation is compared to marriage.

When we drink the Lord's Supper, or partake of Communion, we are affirming that we are committed to Christ; that we have accepted His contract. But Christ added still more to the contract: He called the cup His blood. By accepting His blood, we accept our culpability for His death. We affirm that He died for our sins, and that by sinning, we killed him as surely as if we drove the nails ourselves.

We also take in His blood, and become one with it. We acknowledge that we are to become like Christ, and that Christ is becoming a part of us. From Leviticus, we know that the life is in the blood; by taking in Christ's symbolic blood, we adopt His life. Christ's blood is also our redemption: Without the shedding of blood there is no remission of sin. We not only acknowledge our sin, but its cure as well. In one cup, we are made guilty and cured of guilt; made killers of Christ and grafted to His life; made an enemy of Christ in sin, and made a part of His family by the marriage contract.

The Holy Grail, indeed.

About the Meaning of Life and Argument by Desire

An issue arises here, called "Argument by Desire." C.S. Lewis argued, in some of his books, that our desire for the other-worldly – for intangible things like Love, Joy, Peace, and Heaven – implies that we were designed for a different world than the one in which we live. We live in a world of complex desires that never satisfy us.

We sometimes thirst; this implies that we are creatures who naturally drink water. We hunger; this implies that food is a natural part of our lives. What can we conclude, then, if the desires and thirst of our soul is unattainable in this world?

One of Franz Kafka's greatest stories, called *Before the Law*, tells the tale of a man who spends his life trying to approach a courtroom where he can obtain a just outcome to his case. The intangible thing he desires is unattainable and yet, as he discovers at the end of the story, the entrance where he spent his life in vain was only ever intended for him. In this we see the hopeless desire for something – justice – that we cannot have while we dwell in jars of clay.

And this implies, using the argument by desire, that because we seek justice, and love, and a meaning to life, that we were made for a world in which we can live without clay bodies, and in which the justice and love and meaningful life are all absolute. We may not attain it; that's not implied. But we were made for a different world.

And this further implies what we already know – the thing that crushed poor Franz – that we can never be happy in this life. Is it any wonder that the Bible (Colossians 3:2) tells us to set our eyes on things above?

In chapter six, we mentioned Tolstoy, and how he found the church to be the one bridge between the Finite and the Infinite. We need to understand that he was not saying that the church tells us nice stories about things that we do not understand. He was saying that the fact that there are things beyond us – infinite things, intangible things, numinous things – indicates that there is another world, where those things belong; and only the church can bridge the gap to that other world.

He was arguing for the infinite as evidence of God. C.S. Lewis carried a similar argument even further in his book *The Problem of Pain,* where he says that the existence of pain is evidence that we do not fit this world, and were designed for a different one.

Desire, in that we seek things beyond, and the futility of a world where things beyond are unattainable, and the fact that we need a bridge to those things beyond, and the fact that we suffer and know pain in this world beyond what we can bear – All of these are signs that we are fish out of water. We are out of our element, out of our universe; we are not of this world.

As an aside upon an aside – if we may doubly digress – Lewis had a theory about why we cannot have the ultimate Justice and the ultimate Love and the other intangibles that we seek while we live in these bodies. It is that we, in this flesh, are too weak for them. The intangibles and the infinite would unmake us, were we not transformed. And so, for now, we see through a mirror, darkly; but then, as Paul tells us, we shall see face to face.

---

* The careful reader will find these themes in War and Peace, and Anna Karenina, also. Many of Tolstoy's characters spend their lives searching for a meaning. One might see Natasha Rustova's intellectual and spiritual journey as a foreshadow of Tolstoy's own search, as outlined in Confession. One might draw a parallel between Count Bezhokov's dying despair with Tolstoy's own fear of meaningless death, and in Nikolai Rustov's wartime adventures, or Dolokhov's fantasies of glory, we see a peek at Tolstoy's journey through pointless pseudo-answers.

** The closest Pascal came to actually saying this, so far as anyone can prove, is in *Pensees*, #425. To my knowledge, it has also not been found anywhere in the writings of Calvin, nor in those of Augustine.

CHAPTER NINE

What Is an Atheist, Anyway?

THERE ARE SEVERAL terms related to discussions of atheism, and these terms are not always used correctly. This can lead to a distraction, as the subject of the discussion ceases to be theology and becomes the definitions of words. For example, if we take the strict definition on atheist – from the Greek roots a (no) + Theos (God) – the idea of atheism is absolutely silly. From the etymology, the word should refer to people who believe that there are exactly zero gods in the universe.

We cannot say that a thing definitely does not exist unless we can look everywhere that it might be. I can say that there is not a snowplow in my fireplace by looking into my fireplace – nope, no snowplow. But I can not say that there is no snowplow in any fireplace. There might be a large fireplace and a small snowplow somewhere, and I simply don't know where to look. So to say that there is no god at all is logically absurd.

Most atheists prefer to call those atheists – the ones who refuse to believe in any gods – "strong" atheists, and instead endorse "weak atheism" by which they mean the belief that a god probably does not exist, or that there is no reason to believe in a god. In common parlance, this is sometimes called "agnosticism," but agnosticism comes from the roots a (not) + gnost (to know), and refers to those who believe that whether there is or is not a god cannot be known. One might assume that an agnostic does "not know" if there is a god, but this is incorrect.

One might debate whether it makes sense to believe that the existence of God is not knowable. One might also debate whether answering, "The question cannot be answered" is cheating and a cop-out. But we digress.

Today's atheist will typically say something to the effect that he does not know, but sees no reason to believe that there is a God. Some will even take the position that they are "6/7" certain that there is no god. The practical difference between this position and saying that there is absolutely no god is usually hypothetical, but taking advantage of this difference can allow an atheist to evade the argument.

> **A:** I am an Atheist.
> **C:** Why do you believe that there is no God?
> **A:** Well, that's not what "atheist" means.
> **C:** Actually, the Greek roots are "no" + "God."
> **A:** But it would be silly to believe that there cannot be a god.
> **C:** Well, yes, and that's my point…
> **A:** Atheists just believe in one god less than you do.
> (And thus the argument is about definitions, not about theology).

Since we have broken out the Greek roots, we may as well cover the remaining "-theist" words: A Monotheist believes in exactly one God, a Polytheist believes in many gods, a Henotheist believes that many gods exist, but only worships one of them, and a Pantheist believes that everything and everyone is a part of "god" (by which they mean an impersonal universal life force). Fortunately, no one debates the exact meaning of these words, and that is unlikely to change unless Henotheism becomes a popular lifestyle sometime soon.

Another hair to split is the difference between Deists and Theists. Both come from roots that mean "God-person" (or more loosely translated, "God-believer"). A Theist (from the Greek "theos," meaning god) can be any of the various theistic types – Monothesists, polytheists, and even pantheists. The Deist, however (from the Latin "Dei" meaning "God"), believes that there exists exactly one god, however, the Deist either does not know which god, or else chooses not to inquire further.

Thomas Jefferson is often used as the "poster child" for Deism. Jefferson famously edited a version of the Bible, removing all supernatural references, leaving only practical, historical, and moral teachings. Jefferson apparently believed that he would be judged for his deeds, but did not know by whom.

Some see Deism as a half-step towards Christianity. In his autobiographical *Surprised by Joy; the shape of my early life*, C. S. Lewis remarks upon a motorcycle ride, stating that he got into the sidecar a Deist, and climbed out a Christian, without a clear moment at which he changed his mind. This may be true in some cases, and may not be true in others. Each individual should be considered separately.

Atheists, as we've discussed, sometimes use a twist of definitions to send the argument off onto a tangent. I once had an argument in which I tired of parsing definitions, and created my own terms. I defined an "XYZist" as a person who believed that there exist exactly zero gods, and an "ABCist" as someone who does not know if gods exist, but doesn't believe in any. It took less than five minutes for the atheist to begin arguing that I was using an incorrect definition for XYZist, a word that I had personally made up and defined.

With so many terms to keep track of, and so many shades of definition at hand, what should you do if the person with whom you are speaking begins twisting and chopping definitions, in hopes of catching you off-guard? In the end, the simple course is best. Simply say, "So what do you believe?"

One can then discuss the theological implications of what the person actually believes, rather than the definitions of the words that almost represent the person's system of belief.

CHAPTER TEN

Common Misconceptions about God, Jesus, and Religion

A LARGE PART of atheism is bad religion. It often seems like most atheists became atheists because someone, somewhere, malpracticed his religion. One man who was very dismissive of Christianity told me that as a child in Nebraska, he attended a Methodist church, where the subject of every sermon was the fact that the Methodist minister wasn't paid as well as the Presbyterian minister down the street. To this man, religion was a business: It was the sale of guilt.

You might say that people like this are "inoculated" against religion: they've had just enough to render them immune. Of course, we know that Christianity is not for sale, nor is it about guilt. In fact, True Religion frees us from guilt. We need look no further than Isaiah 1:18 to see it: "Come, let us counsel together, saith the Lord: Though your sins be as scarlet, they shall be whiter than snow; though they be red like crimson, they shall be as wool."

The Bible does teach that we are guilty of sin, but only because that teaching is a pre-requisite to the forgiveness of sin. The book of Romans tells us exactly this: that the Law was our schoolmaster

– the servant whose job was to oversee the education of the children in a wealthy household. We were supposed to learn from the law, first that we were in violation of God's law, and secondly that we could not, of our own, do anything about that. The Bible further teaches that salvation is a gift (Romans 6:23) and that it comes by grace (Ephesians 2:8-9), and grace is getting what we don't deserve.

That Christianity is about guilt is a misconception – a lie, actually – meant to scare us away from Christ. Christianity is not about guilt, but about grace.

This also answers the argument that God is standing above us with a bag on anvils, waiting for us to screw up so that He can drop one of those anvils on our heads. God is not shocked by our sins. He knows our heart of hearts – read Psalm 139 if you doubt it. He died to fix us. He expended the very blood of Heaven's Prince for our salvation, demonstrating both the seriousness of our sin and the wonderful depths of the love that He has towards us: "But God demonstrates His love toward us in this: While we were still sinners, Christ died for us."

The misconception of God as an angry avenger of trivial mistakes is based on another misconception, which is that the God of the Old Testament is different from the God of the New Testament. This in turn usually bases itself on the destruction of Canaanite tribes, or the purging of the camp after the Golden Calf event after Moses obtained the Ten Commandments from God at Mount Sinai.

To use these passages to indite God for cruelty requires taking them out of context and ignoring God's attempts to prevent these events. We are expressly told, in Genesis, that the Israelites will spend 430 years in Egypt because the sins of the Amorites were not yet complete. That is, that the people living in the Promised Land had not yet reached a degree of depravity for which God was willing to end them. By the time God was willing to write them off they had reached heights of depravity that would make Sodom blush.

Examples of God showing mercy include His decision not to destroy Ninevah in Jonah's day, based upon their repentance (and this is the real point of the story, not the bit with the fish). God stated that His reason for wanting Ninevah to repent, and not to be destroyed, was that there were innocents in Ninevah, alongside the depraved.* This is not consistent with a God who is waiting, on bated breath, to drop hammers on our heads.

The God of the New Testament extends this same mercy to those who ask it. The God who released the woman caught in the act of adultery is the same God who rescued Rahab from Jericho. The same God who told us to love our enemies in the Sermon on the Mount is the same God who forced Jonah to rescue the Ninevites. The same God who heard the pleas of the Centurion, and of the Syrio-Phoenician woman, is the God who heard the cries of the Hebrews in Egypt.

To say that these are not the same God is to ignore virtually the entire Bible.

Another misconception about God is to believe that He is distant, and that He doesn't concern Himself with individuals. The Bible is full of passages that contradict this idea. God calls for us to "counsel together" with Him (Isaiah 1:18). He becomes a living Human, subject to human frailty and emotion, and "Pitches his tent among us" (a literal translation of John 1:14: "The Word became flesh, and dwelt among us…"), which is to remind us of the tabernacle in the wilderness, in the center of the camp, where God's presence was visible as a pillar of cloud and fire. That God is personal, and seeks us as individual persons, to whom He will relate one-on-one, is inescapable.

We see Abraham, with whom God shared His counsels on the Plains of Mamre. We see David, whom God called a man after God's own heart. We see the three Friends of Daniel, with whom the Son of God walked in the fire. One of God's names, Emmanuel, means "God with us."

God went so far as to walk alongside Galilean fishermen, breaking bread with publicans, healing the sick, and teaching the masses. God could not have been more personal and closer to us.

God's compassion is illustrated very clearly in John 11:35. "Jesus wept" for Lazarus, his friend who had died, and this despite the fact that, moments later, He would raise him from the dead. Witnesses to the scene said to each other, "See how he loved him?" and when we consider the cross, we should say, "See how he loves us?" God is not distant. He is as near as our prayers.

Another misconception is to think that if something is mentioned in the Bible, it must therefore be an example to be followed. The error here is that the Bible writers expected us to know right from wrong. They assumed that we did not need a running commentary, and that to describe the deed was to give us all the moral background that we need.

This can be misapplied in several ways. We can hear it said that Laban had household idols and therefore we should also (this neglects that Laban was a pagan, ignorant of God's nature and laws). Or we may hear it said that "Jesus arose a long time before dawn" and that therefore we must also.

Lacking a moral index in the passage, such as that God judged the individual for the act, we must not be hasty in assuming any act to be a good or bad example. In general, we can assume that any act of Jesus is morally correct – We know that He "was tempted in all ways, like as we, yet without sin." But that doesn't mean that we are compelled to drive animals out of temples, or to curse fig trees.

It is not okay to have household idols just because Laban did it, nor to steal them from pagans because Rachel did, nor to cheat your brother because Jacob did. Here, as in all Bible passages, context is everything.

We cannot leave this subject without touching on what is probably the most common misconception of all: That we will eventually be judged on the net balance of our good and our evil deeds. This is not what the Bible teaches at all. The Bible teaches that we have all done wrong, and that to claim never to have done wrong is to call God a liar.

The Bible teaches that there is a punishment that not only follows from that wrong, but is actually a part of it and a natural consequence of it, just as to burn your skin is a natural consequence of touching fire. The Bible says that death is the Wages of our Sin – the payback that we have earned by sinning. The Bible says that we will be judged for our sins.

Imagine a man going before a judge and saying, "Your honor, I admit that I stole this car and ran a red light. But I had just rescued a basket of kittens from drowning, and had given my entire paycheck to the Salvation Army.**" How would the judge respond? Would he find that the good deeds outweighed the bad?

If he were a good judge, he would ignore the good deeds and judge you according to the bad deeds, as justice demands. And God is the ultimately Good Judge. He is the author of Justice. And in the end, Justice will be done.

Romans 6:23 sums it up: "The wages of sin is death, but the gift of God is eternal life through Jesus Christ our Lord."

You are familiar with wages. Wages are earned. You have worked to receive them. They are a natural consequence for your labor, and they are linked together. The wage-giver is obligated by law to see that you receive your wages on payday, and that you receive the proper wages at the proper time.

The wages of sin is death. Death here refers to the second death, or Hell. We have earned it. We have worked to receive it. It will be a natural consequence of the things that we have done. On the pay day – the Last Day, the Day of Judgment – we will surely and definitely receive what is due us.

But the gift of God is eternal life. Quite the opposite here: We can't have death and eternal life at the same time, can we? To receive this gift would obviously help us to avoid a paycheck that we really do not want.

A gift is not earned. If it could be earned, it would be wages. A gift is not something that we deserve. A gift is not a natural consequence of our actions. We have not worked to receive it. It is not given from an obligation, but from Free Will. A gift comes from Love – every true gift that you have ever received has been a consequence of someone's love for you.

God's gift (it follows) is a consequence of His love for you, and Romans 5:8 affirms this. Further, in Ephesians 2:8-9, we find that it is by Grace that we are saved, and that not of ourselves; it is a gift of God, lest any man should boast. So it cannot be good deeds, or a balance of your virtues against your vices, which save you.

It is a gift of God: His unmerited Grace and Mercy.

Before we go any further, it would help to define Grace: Grace is when we get something that we don't deserve. In contrast, Mercy is when we don't get what we do deserve.

As we think about a gift, we should also consider that the giving of a gift is a two-part transaction: the gift must be given and also received. It does us no good to have been offered God's Gift of Eternal Life if we ignore it and do not receive it. So how can we dodge our wages, which we rightly deserve, and receive God's gift, which we do not deserve?

Through Jesus Christ, our Lord. In John 1:10-12, we see the importance of receiving Christ: He was in the world, and the world was made by Him, but the world did not know Him. He came to His own people, but His own people did not receive Him. But to as many as received Him, to them He gave the power to become sons of God, even to as many as believed on His Name. Through Christ, we are able to receive the gift and lose the wages. ***

We need to first Admit that we have done wrong. We need to agree with God that we have sinned against Him. Then we need to Believe that Jesus Christ died for our sins. Finally, we need to Commit our lives to Him.

This can be done in a brief prayer, along the lines of:

Lord Jesus,

I know that I am a sinner and have done wrong things. I am sorry for my sins, and I ask you for the free gift of eternal life, and that you will save me from the wages of my sins. I thank you for your sacrifice for me, and I thank you for your mercy. I commit myself to following you, and ask that you guide my life and become my Lord. I call upon Your Name for my salvation.

In Your Name, Amen.

It's that simple: we will not be judged by our works, nor by some cosmic balance of good and bad karma, but by whether we have clung to our sins and demanded our wages, or have trusted Jesus Christ to do it all for us.

There's a lot more to be said on the question of Works and Grace, and some people have the misconception that Paul (who wrote about Grace) and James (who wrote about works) were teaching different and contrary doctrines. In fact, the two apostles do not contradict each other at all. Paul tells us that Works do not save us, and James tells us that Good Works will grow from the fact that we have been saved.

Works do not and cannot save us. As Augustus Toplady wrote in the hymn, *Rock of Ages, Cleft for Me*, "Not the labors of my hands could fulfil the law's demands; these for sin could not atone; Thou must save and thou alone; In my hand no price I bring, simply to Thy cross I cling."

I am certain that both James and Paul could sing that old hymn together in perfect harmony.

One final misconception is that Hell will be a place of partying and wild frivolity. This idea is usually expressed flippantly, through remarks such as, "Hell's gonna have all the best music" or "We're so bad, we'll take the place over!" This is a dangerous misconception. Hell, regardless of who is there, or what characteristics they may have, will not be a place for parties.

The Bible describes it as a place of misery, and of wailing and gnashing of teeth. Jesus told a parable about Hell in which a man there wished for a single drop of cold water on the tip of his tongue. Considering how tiny is the tip of one's tongue, and how little relief a single drop of water would provide, the misery of Hell must be nearly infinite. Hell in the Bible is always compared to unquenchable fires, unending pain, and mental anguish.

Some Bible scholars have argued that Hell's worst aspect will not be any physical punishment, but simply that one will be completely separated from God. To these writers – the curious may wish to consider C. S. Lewis' *The Great Divorce* – the misery comes from within, as one must listen to one's own whining and excuse-making for all of eternity.

Whatever the case, the idea of ruling Hell, or of overcoming the unpleasant aspects to enjoy the fellowship of friends – that's simply absurd. The residents of Hell will not be able to enjoy anything, because they sacrificed all real joy on the altar of Self. They will not be able to enjoy friends, nor will they have the mental strength to overcome their own obsessions with themselves. They will be lost.

Lewis even argued that by the time a person commits himself to Hell, there is nothing left that could be called humanity, as the person will have become merely a whining remnant of himself, more whine than self. If you think about it, you may know people who have already begun their hell here on earth, because their self-pity and whining have trumped everything else in their lives.

Fire or no fire, Hell is a horrible place. I beg you, in the Name of God's Son, Jesus, not to go there.

---

* We wrongly assume that the book of Jonah was a fish story. In fact, the book of Jonah is about God's mercy. God goes to great length to explain His mercy to Jonah, who would rather die than to give the Ninevites a chance to repent. Jonah grieves more for a vine that shades him than for a city of hundreds of thousands. Perhaps we simply do not understand the depth and breadth of God's mercy.

** By the way, while giving an entire paycheck would be a bit over the top, I do advocate gifts for the Salvation Army, a worthy organization if ever there was one. At the very least, empty your change jar into a red kettle next Christmas, won't you?

*** For this simple and elegant explanation of Romans 6:23, I am indebted to R.R., M.Div., whom I have been privileged to call (at various times) my pastor, mentor, teacher, and friend.

CHAPTER ELEVEN

Other Arguments That You May Hear

IN A WORLD where misconceptions about God outnumber doctrines, any number of specious arguments about God may exist as well. We'll look at a couple of them, in order to practice taking apart these arguments as well. The difference here is that, unlike atheists, the originator of these arguments does not intend to destroy your faith, but to bend it towards his religious position. Some of these people are our Christian brothers. Others are pretenders and fakes.

Discernment and careful thinking can help us keep from being deceived or drawn into an extremist position. Typically, these arguments begin with a reasonable premise, such as noting that Jesus ate figs, then progress to less reasonable premises, such as that therefore figs are good, therefore fig cookies are the only holy food.

The progression is from something which the Bible appears to either prescribe or proscribe, through interim steps, to something currently affecting our everyday lives. We start with the fact that Jesus drove moneychangers from the temple, and we derive from that the church cannot take offerings during church services; and in deriving our false conclusion, we lose the context and we lose the underlying principle.

There are also spurious arguments that hinge upon "proof-texting" or taking a single verse out of context in order to make an argument. For example, I once had a man use Philippians 2:5-6 to "prove" that we can become Gods. In order to make his case, however, he had to ignore… The context, the context, the context. Phil. 2:3 sets the tone by stressing humility. If we continue the sentence which begins "Have this mind in you which was also in Christ Jesus: Who being in the form of God, thought it not robbery to be equal with God:" (vv. 5&6, where my friend would have had me stop) we find, "But made Himself of no reputation, and took upon Him the form of a servant, and was made in the likeness of men: And being found in fashion as a man, He humbled Himself and became obedient unto death, even the death of the cross." (vv. 7-8).

Whoops. In context, the passage is not telling us that we should aspire to become gods, but that we should imitate the humility of Christ. The reference to His deity and his equality with God is merely to show us how far He lowered Himself.

While we are on the subject, it is noteworthy to consider the amazing humility of Jesus Christ. He was God, Creator of all things, and made Himself into a man. That in itself is a huge step down, but He also became a servant among men – The Creator God washed the stinky feet of Galilean fishermen! – and then went further, to die horribly, wrongly accused, in painful and cruel humiliation among thieves who were actually guilty. All of that, for my sins. For yours.

What the angels must have thought, to see their King, the holy Ancient of Days, being bruised, bloodied, and nailed to a cross! We cannot imagine the horror and confusion that they must have felt.

That thought bears further contemplation.

But not all arguments are so easy to deflate. Some have raged for centuries, such as the debate between Free Will and Predestinationism. And in the Free Will question, there are good and righteous people on either side of the debate.

The issue hinges upon whether we choose to have faith in Jesus Christ, and thus are saved by our Free Will choice; or if we are incapable of any good choice, and are saved by God's fiat, through an irresistible grace that compels us to have faith in God. One side contends that Jesus died for all mankind, and that whosoever will may come, and the other side contends that Christ died only for those whom God chose, and that salvation is a matter of acknowledging the inevitable regeneration.

One should quickly note that the point is largely moot. We have been saved; we know this. How we came to be saved is beside the point. Did we choose God, or did He choose us? Well, the fact is that we and God agree that we are sinners, and that His Son died to atone for our sins. We agree that our faith is in Christ alone, by His Grace alone and our Faith alone.

Whether we take the James Harmon position – that Christ died for all, and that we freely choose Him – or the John Calvin position – that we were predestined to submit to His irresistible grace – we remain Christians, and we may find this debate still raging in heaven. We will certainly meet people in Heaven with whom we closely contested the issue.

My own position on the matter is a modified Arminian position: I believe that we are saved by Free Will, but I disagree with Harmon on the matter of Security of the Believer. I believe that once we are saved, we are saved forever, because the images that the Bible uses to describe Salvation are of adoption, marriage, and new birth. All of these are permanent changes, meant to endure. One may die, but one cannot be unborn; One may divorce, but one cannot be unmarried, just as a bell cannot be unrung.

I mention the Calvinist/Arminian debate to emphasize that there are some arguments that we don't need to argue. If we were to sway a Calvinist to Arminianism, we would not be leading him into Heaven. If we were to persuade an Arminian to accept the Security of the Believer, we might give him more confidence in his eternal security, but we would not be leading him to Christ.

In this matter, it would be best to agree to disagree, and to extricate ourselves from the argument. That's not always easy to do. I spent much of fifth and sixth grades arguing for the Security of the Believer with two classmates who were of the full Arminian persuasion. In retrospect, we were all merely parroting the arguments of our elders, of course.

I suppose that the best things for us to take from this chapter as it pertains to the Calvinist / Arminian / Modified Arminian debate would be:

1. It is not always necessary to argue the point, and
2. It is not always necessary to know everything, and
3. A person can vehemently disagree with doctrines that you hold near and dear, yet still not be your enemy.

This raises another point about doctrine: Some doctrines are intrinsic, and others are arbitrary. In a Systematic Theology course that I attended, many years ago, the professor raised this distinction with regards to salvation. He felt that the method of our Salvation, which is the death, burial, and resurrection of Jesus Christ, was not arbitrary – God did not decide to save us that way just because it seemed like a good idea. He reasoned that Christ's death was necessary for our atonement.

An analogy that he used was a man trapped in a burning building: If we imagine a man in a burning house, who is unable to reach the door, what advice might we give him? We could tell him to crawl to the kitchen and eat crackers and wine. We could tell him to go to the sink and sprinkle water on himself. We could tell him to do good works. But in the end, what the man needs is for someone to take an ax and to bash a hole in the wall, so that he can crawl out.

The ax and the hole are intrinsic to the rescue – they are vital parts which cannot be removed from it. The other things – sprinkling water, drinking wine, doing good works – those may be important at other times, but they are arbitrary with regards to his immediate salvation from this particular fire. In regards to our own sin, at a certain point Jesus had to do the thing intrinsic to our rescue, which was to be crucified for our sins.

Another analogy – my own; I'm not even sure Dr. G. played card games – is a card trick. The trickster does many things – his hands are in motion and seem to never stop. Some of these actions are intrinsic to the trick, such as having the victim select a card, or having a means to find that card again for the end. Other things, such as shuffling the deck, waving the deck in the air, offering to cut the deck, etc., are merely there to distract. They are a part of the trick, because if only the intrinsic parts were shown, we'd know how it's done. But they don't have to be done that particular way, or in any particular order. They are arbitrary.

We can apply this idea far more broadly than Dr. G. ever intended: Some parts of anything are intrinsic, and others arbitrary. An automobile has intrinsic parts – an engine, a transmission, a drive train, wheels, brakes, seats, a means of steering and control – and arbitrary parts, such as the fenders, the hood ornament, or the hub caps. Even within the engine, some parts are arbitrary, such as the means of aspiration – we can use a carburetor, or a port fuel injection system, or a cylinder injection system, with or without a blower, or a turbocharger, and so on.

Note that "arbitrary" does not mean "unnecessary." We must have some means of aspiration: A car will not run without a proper mixture of fuel and air. But it is not necessary to choose any one of these methods in order to make the car run; each will work just as well as the others (well, actually, each has advantages and disadvantages, but that's not the point). In the card trick, the arbitrary portions serve a purpose, but they need not be those particular arbitrary portions.

With that in mind, we should careful consider the Calvinist / Arminian question again: Is it intrinsic that my Christian Brother believe in the Security of the Believer in order for him to be saved? Obviously not: It is intrinsic to our faith – vital, central, undeniable core doctrine – that Christ died for our sins. Whether He did so for all men (and only some accept that gift) or for only those whom He knew in advance would accept – that question is arbitrary (because either belief will still bring the same result: Saving faith in Jesus Christ).

Equally important, however, is the converse of this point: Not everyone who agrees with us (or appears to) on one issue agrees with us on all. Just because a person claims to be a Christian, or uses sacred-speak, we should not therefore assume him or her to be a Christian. There are wolves in sheep's clothing lurking in every field.

As an example, many businesses place an ichthys symbol on their business signs or business cards. Some are actually Christians, and operate their business by principles that Jesus Christ would approve. Others use the symbol to lure in Christians by making them think the businessman is "one of us."

I have become leery of doing business where I see an ichthys, because it often means, "I expect my customers to ignore unprofessional or dishonest conduct, because wink-wink we're all on the same team here, wink-wink." This is not an absolute rule, of course, but it bears consideration.

There is nothing wrong with the ichthys symbol itself – two opposing curves overlaid so that the result vaguely resembles a fish – and it was used in ancient times as a means for Christians to identify each other despite oppression. The Greek word "Ichthys" – Iota, Chi, Theta, Upsilon, Sigma – means "fish" and is also an acronym for the Greek words, "Jesus Christ, God's Son, Savior." Thus the fish symbol represents Jesus.

The error comes in the assumption that the ichthys symbol always denotes a Christian. When we are confronted by a person who claims to be a Christian, we should be able to identify them by certain things, such as Christian behavior, Christian charity, honesty, kindness, and a strong work ethic. "By their fruit," Jesus told us, "Shall ye know them."

One man whom I knew could not speak without adding "Brother" to his sentences. There is nothing wrong with the title, and there is no reason not to apply it to Christian brethren. But if a man – as this one did – peppers his speech too heavily with the word, it should make you ask, "Why is this man working so hard to remind me of our common faith?"

In this man's case, those who knew his business practices had good reason to question his Christianity – the "fruits" of his life did not agree with his claims to Christian faith. As a general rule now, if a man calls me "Brother" while we discuss a Bible study, I smile and call him "Brother." If a man calls me "Brother," or otherwise makes a point of reminding me of my faith, during a business transaction, I politely excuse myself.

Should the question arise on the internet, there are ways to challenge a person to reveal whether he or she is truly a Christian. One method is to ask him to tell you his salvation experience. A true testimony will usually be in the form of, "My life was like this, and then I met Jesus, and He changed me thus, and now God is doing this in my life."

A testimony that recites a laundry list of sins, and then ends with, "And then I found Jesus and now I'm all good" should raise red flags because the emphasis is on the sin, and not its cure. A testimony that is vague, such as "Well, you know, God's like my father, you know," suggests that the person never had a moment when he deliberately chose to follow Christ. This is a matter for discernment – it may be that the person simply does not know how to express what happened when Christ entered His life – but in hearing a testimony, one should listen for things that ring true in one's own experience.

Often – but not always – when speaking to a Christian, there will be a certain tugging in your heart, almost like a resonance within you. This may be the Holy Spirit confirming to you that the other person is a Christian. There may be certain statements that make sense to you, as a Christian, but not to a non-Christian. Once, in an internet discussion forum, I had a conversation with an atheist – it was on the question of whether it is a good thing to follow instructions one believes came from God – and it went something like this:

> **Atheist:** Suppose that someone told you that God ordered him to rob a bank and to shoot people. What would you do? Would you help him? What if that was God's Will? *
>
> **Me:** I would ask him to explain why he thought God had told him that, and I would pray that God would confirm to me whether God had given him this instruction. It's unlikely that God said that, of course, since it's contrary to God's character. But if He did, then the Spirit in me would agree with the Spirit in him.
>
> **Atheist:** So you know what God has said to other people?
>
> **Me:** Sometimes, yes; we call it discernment, and sometimes there's a word of knowledge or a word of wisdom…
>
> **Atheist:** How long have you had this magic superpower?
>
> **Me:** Since 1972.

The atheist had no reply, but a fellow Christian on the forum replied with laughter at the Atheist's confusion.

Then the fellow Christian added, "For me, it was 1973." Clearly, the atheist did not understand that the indwelling Spirit is One God, and not a haphazard set of feelings that change as often as the wind blows. We had a good laugh at the Atheist's expense, and he left wondering what was so funny.

Of course, if there hadn't been a Christian brother there to affirm what I was saying, then the Atheist would have claimed that I was lying, or written me off as delusional. But we Christians, whatever our denomination or creed, serve One God. That God is a God of order, and not chaos; and His Spirit dwells within us. We should look to that Spirit when we hear someone make claims that do not match the Word, God's Nature, and confirmation through prayer.

As an example of how this works, I once heard a man stand up in a class full of mature Christians and say, "The Lord told me that I'm supposed to go on a missions trip to Russia."

Faced with this bombshell, we began to look for confirmation that God had told him this. One means of confirming such a thing – confirming that it came from God, and not our feelings – is to seek the counsel of Godly friends. Had he spoken to friends about it?

Everyone he had told had doubted him. This was a bad indication. We also doubted.

God speaks through circumstances. Did he know anyone in Russia? Did he have means to get there? Was he working with a mission-sending organization?

No. Circumstances were against him, as well.

God prepares people, and shapes them to the tasks before them. Did he speak Russian? Was he studying Russian? Did he know anything about Russian culture? No to all.

God speaks through His Word, and through prayer. This man claimed that his prayers and Bible reading had led him to this conclusion. He was adamant. But the Spirit within us did not agree with him. We unanimously felt that he was mistaken.

Eventually, the appointed time came, and he quit his job, waiting for God to miraculously teleport him to Red Square. It didn't happen. He did get evicted for non-payment of rent, but that only took him to the curb. I think we can say that God had nothing to do with that man's "revelation."

This is the discernment that I tried in vain to describe to the atheist; all of us in the room knew that this young man was not going to Russia.

To try to summarize this point: We should not jump to conclusions about a person's faith, or lack thereof, based solely upon what they say and how they say it. We need to analyze not only what a person claims, but the person's deeds, the person's character, and what the Spirit of God tells us about the person. Many people have been led astray by false pastors who said the right words for the wrong purposes. Beware.

---

* This question was a trap, of course. If I had said that I would automatically believe anyone who claimed a revelation from God, then the Atheist would have argued that I should accept any number of obviously false "revelations" and any number of false prophets, thus reducing my position to absurdity; If I had said that I would automatically reject it, then I would be contradicting my prior statements that God speaks to men. This question is also an "improper question" because it assumes two contradictory things: The God we know, and that God's nature was ungodly. Clearly, this is a contradiction in terms.

CHAPTER TWELVE

Atheism and Ethics

WHEN WE OPEN this can of worms, they tend to wriggle in certain directions: Theists tend to immediately argue that atheism led to Hitler's Germany, Stalin's Russia, and Pol Pot's Cambodia. Atheists argue that Hitler was an altar boy, and that Stalin belonged to the church as a boy; they then imply that all the evils of the world are the fault of religion. The argument is absurd, of course. As we've said before, the failure of one Christian to adhere to the tenets of Christianity does not imply that Christianity is at fault. Instead, it suggests that the Christian is at fault – which, coincidentally, is precisely what Romans 3:10 tells us.

But raising questions of Hitler, Stalin, or Pol Pot tends to create an emotional and divisive distraction from the real point: If there is no God, then there is no basis for morality. The atheist bristles at such a thought. Are we saying that one cannot be moral and still be an atheist?

No, of course not. Obviously an atheist can follow a set of moral rules and comply with social expectations. An atheist can even feel offended and sickened by the egregious violation of the mores he accepts. The argument is not that atheists are immoral. It is that atheists have no basis for their morality.

The atheist will point to artificial moral constructs, such as Kant's Categorial Imperative. A German named Immanuel Kant wrote a book called *Critique of Pure Reason,* and in it he laid down a moral rule that one should only do those things that one is willing to make into a rule for everyone to do. This is his "Categorical Imperative" – Categorical because it applies universally, and Imperative because it must be done in order to be moral, in Kant's opinion.

At first, Kant's Imperative seems like a powerful rule: Only do something if you wish others would do the same thing. Don't steal unless you want everyone to steal, and if you want not to be assaulted, don't assault anyone. But this merely means that if we wish to indulge our vices, we must allow others to indulge theirs. If we don't mind that the neighbors rob banks, we can rob banks.

Part of the mistake here is to assume that society as a whole is a reasonable guide to the behavior of individuals. People are no less sinful as a group than they are separately. As an example, let us take the Caribbe tribe and apply Kant's Categorical Imperative to them.

The Caribbes, for whom the Caribbean Sea was named, are now extinct, and not a moment too soon. They were the cannibals from whom Daniel Dafoes' character, Robinson Crusoe, saved his companion, Friday. Eating their enemies was the least of their sins.

If we apply Kant's Categorical Imperative to the Caribbes – that is, if the Caribbes were to try to apply it to each other – it would be no bar to cannibalism. We quickly see that Kant's

Categorical Imperative can be reduced to a more common rule: "Comply with the societal norm," or "When in Rome, do as the Romans do."

This leads us to another false foundation upon which atheists attempt to build their moral house of cards: Social Contract. The basic idea of a Social contract is that we each agree to surrender certain rights, and to give up certain actions, in order to form a society. In such a case, morality is keeping the contract. Thus we can say that it is immoral for a citizen of New York City to eat his neighbor because it violates the Social Contract of New York, but it was not immoral for the Caribbes to perform the exact same act, because it was not part of their social contract.

You see the problem, of course. Once again, we've made morality a matter of our preferences. Morals, in an atheistic world, boil down to, "I don't like it when people do that." However, if we make morals a matter of preference, then we can evade morals at will. We can eventually twist the shadow of justification around ourselves, until "moral" means "things that I do" and "immoral" means "things that you do."

Earlier, we spoke of those who would find God cruel or unjust for various reasons. When we see that human morality, without God, is a matter of preferences, we understand that to judge God according to our preferences is absurd on the face of it. To call God cruel because someone died is no less silly than to say that we think God is immoral because He doesn't recycle plastics. We are merely saying, "I don't like what God does," even if we pretend that we base it on something.

To put this in different terms: Either God exists, in which case He is the guide to moral behavior, and our preferences, our social contracts and our moral imperatives are meaningless vanity; or else God does not exist, in which case our preferences, social contracts and moral imperatives are mere vanity. In neither case can a man find God to be immoral; In neither case is there a standard of justice that applies to God.

An atheist does not come easily to this position. He will argue for the overall moral progress of mankind, such that we now recognize the immorality of more savage times. This is absurd, of course; mankind as a whole is no less brutal than at any time in the past. If anything, we have found new ways to multiply our brutality.

The atheist will argue that we all know what morals are, and thus we need no formal code of conduct to guide us. Again, this is absurd. If morals are objective and universal, then they come from somewhere outside of our own lives, which implies God; and if morals are subjective then we do need a formal code of conduct, to be certain that we all have the same code. It does us no good to be moral and ethical if others will not do likewise.

An honest atheist, at this point, will grudgingly concede that morals, if there is no God, are nothing more than a statement of preferences. We prefer that people behave in such-and-such a manner, and thus it is "right" and to behave contrary to that is "wrong." The atheist may grasp at a few straws, such as the claim that the consensus of us all is stronger than the opinions of each of us individually.

This is another unfounded idea. The fact that we consent to a set of rules, or that we express our preferences corporately instead of individually makes no differences: a godless moral code remains a statement of preferences.

We need to be careful here: We are not saying that an atheist cannot be moral. We are saying that the moral codes followed by atheists are merely statements of preferences. So why is this important?

In the chapter concerning arguments against Christianity, we only touched lightly on a class of arguments that I refer to as "God is mean" arguments. These go further than the "Why would a loving God do (or permit) X?" arguments that we mentioned. These arguments generally start with the mention of some perceived atrocity in the Old Testament, and then use these to assault the character of God. It's usually phrased something like, "Your God is a murderer."

As you can see, that claim is absurd on several levels for several reasons, including that murder is an unlawful killing, and no law applies to God. Further, of course, the ending of life is God's exclusive domain.

Sometimes, atheists will concede that morals not rooted in God are entirely subjective – mere expressions of preferences – and will say things like "See, we can make up morals and follow them without needing God to tell us what's moral."

Well, yes, but that wasn't the question. And even if it were, the idea that we don't need God in order to learn and follow morals contains a false assumption, namely, that the point of the Bible and Christianity was to teach us morals. Nothing could be further from the truth. The purpose of the Law was to teach us that we can not be moral. We are all sinners, as we see in Romans 3:10 and 3:23. We need God's grace, which is the central lesson of the Gospels.

In general, Ethics and Morals arguments – the ones that dodge the Stalin/Hitler/Pol Pot pitfall – almost always hinge upon an ambiguous definition, or a misunderstanding. There is a tendency in arguments with atheists for them to hear (regardless what you might have said) that you think they are immoral. Atheists tend to be sensitive to judgment, even if they are not actually being judged.

CHAPTER THIRTEEN

Order of Battle

NOW, LET US consider the Order of battle. Order of battle, as used by military men, means either the order in which a General brings his forces to bear, or else the analysis of the forces and resources available in battle. We shall use it in the former sense.

It may happen that you pass an idle afternoon over coffee with a friend, and the subject turns to spiritual things. Or perhaps you overhear two coworkers, one a wolf and one a sheep, as the former tries to lead the latter into a philosophical blunder. It might be that you have challenged some atheist, or you might have been minding your own business when you are beset by wolves. In any case, the battle begins when an idea is presented that is contrary to the Bible, logic, and good reasoning.

It is rare for ideas to be presented frankly and forthrightly, especially fatally flawed ideas, and that is why you will need skill and discernment to carve bad arguments apart. The first point in the order of battle must therefore be to ask yourself whether you are prepared to engage this enemy. If you are not, then withdraw at once.

Preparation is not a simple thing. Remember that when Jesus sent the disciples out, casting demons from those afflicted with them, he told them that some required special preparation: "This kind comes not out except with much prayer and fasting." To be prepared for an intellectual battle, you must be prepared. Prayer is the first step, so listen to the Spirit, to see if He will tell you to engage or to withdraw. Consider whether you have armed yourself according to Paul's instructions, in Ephesians:

1. *Surrounded with the belt of truth*: If you put forward lies – making up outrageous stories of your conversion, for example, or citing something that someone told you that they read happened to some missionary or another – you leave yourself vulnerable.

2. *Having shod your feet with the preparation of the gospel of peace:* If you go in barefooted, vulnerable, and with your emotions exposed, you can be wounded by the harsh and uncaring words of the opponent. Resolve instead that you will be thick-skinned, like a man with a thick-soled shoe, when you go to battle. Barbs and thorns in the dirt will not scratch you.

3. *Bearing the breastplate of righteousness:* No attack of the enemy is more deadly to our argument than unrighteousness. If you have just been cruel and hurtful, to suddenly say that you are a Christian and to begin defending the Cause of Christ will make you sound hypocritical and insincere. No one will believe you, and you might as well talk to the wall.

4. *Wearing the helmet of salvation:* I cannot overstress this point. To defend Christ, you must first know Christ. Those who know Him not only have the strong assurance of His presence and His help, but also have the Indwelling Spirit of God within them.

5. *Taking up the shield of faith:* You must know what you believe and why you believe it, to prevent some fast talker from persuading you that what you believe is false or somehow invalid. Job said, "I know that my Redeemer lives, and that He shall stand upon the Earth at the last day; I shall see Him with my own eyes." You need to have that sort of assurance, so that the "fiery darts of the evil one" will be quenched.

6. *You need the sword, which is the Word of God.* It is not enough to merely have a Bible: You must know your Bible. You must know what it says, and what it does not say. You must be ready to answer a spurious claim with, "Show me chapter and verse, please," which, surprisingly often, often ends some very ridiculous claims about the Bible. As a soldier practices with his sword (or his rifle) until it becomes like an extension of his arm, so you need to read and practice with your Bible, until you understand its subtle nuances, and the words for the Spirit to bring to your mind are already hidden in your heart.

Having made preparation for battle, and choosing to engage, you must next consider the argument that is presented to you. Scan it first, to find:

1). What it claims – what statements of apparent fact does it make? Does it say that Christ went down to India and studied with Buddha? That would be a claim to challenge: Ask for chapter and verse. Look for any false premise, or for any premise that requires an unsupported assumption by the opponent.

2). What conclusion it tries to make – is the point that Jesus was just a man? Is the point that Jesus never truly lived? Is the point that … Well, what's the "Therefore" or the "So you see..." at the end of the argument?

Next, examine the argument a second time, this time looking for the argument proper. You may wish to lay the argument into a syllogism, so that the form of the argument is obvious. Does it follow a logical form? Does it use words ambiguously?

You may have to read the argument a couple of times to find the false element. Always keep in mind that an argument that reaches an incorrect conclusion – for example, that Jesus was only one of many good moral teachers throughout history – must have a false premise, a conclusion that doesn't follow, or an ambiguity. These false elements may be hidden in assumptions that are not stated clearly.

Remember to ask yourself, What does this really mean? And What does this really prove?

Next, state what you have found, clearly and simply. You may have to say, "Look, in the first sentence, you're using this word to mean one thing, but at the end, you're using it to mean another." Try to be both precise and concise. Remember that Atheists tend to have short attention spans.

The opponent will rebut your points. He may follow any of several strategies:

1.) He may argue in support of his assertions (He may, for example, present some spurious pseudo-gospel or gnostic writing as "Evidence" that Jesus went to India and met Buddha).

2.) He may argue that his errors of logic are not errors.

3.) He may dispute matters of fact.

4.) He may say that your corrections are right, but not important.

5.) He may bring up an unrelated subject in an attempt to distract you.

With any evidence that the opponent presents, you should immediately ask yourself:

1.) Is this true? And

2.) What does this prove?

If you are not certain whether it is true, check the presented facts. Look up the sources – he may be citing only selected parts of an article, or a minority view of an historical event, or he may be lying outright. Then put the fact into perspective: How is it relevant to the argument? If it is true that Napoleon had a snuff-box made of his horse's hoof, does that actually prove that the horse once stepped on his foot? Or is the opponent filling in unknowns – how Napoleon felt towards his horse, and whether the snuffbox was merely a souvenir or was a sign of spite, in this case – with assumptions and unsupported assertions?

Remember to winnow the wheat from the chaff. Separate the argument itself from the flowery words into which the opponent may couch them. There is an extremely funny scene in C. S. Lewis' book, *Out of the Silent Planet*, involving just such a translation. The hero, Dr. Elwin Ransom, has been kidnapped and taken to Mars by two other Earthmen. In time, all three of them are captured and taken before the ruler of Mars. Because the ruler of Mars has become acquainted with Ransom, he permits Ransom to translate for him as he examines the other Earthmen.

Doctor Weston, the more evil of the Earthmen, presents a rousing and inspirational defense of his attempt to mine gold and take it back to Earth, and of his hopes that Mankind may colonize many other planets, reaching to the stars with golden aspirations and similar flowery language. Ransom, however, has only learned a little bit of the Martian language, and has to reduce the statements to their logical cores in order to state them to the Martian ruler. Not only is the result amusing, but it also demonstrates how a ridiculous idea can be made to sound reasonable with pleasant words.

We want always to be Ransom, tearing the meaning from flowery phrases and putting it into simple terms for our own understanding, so that the errors may be revealed.

Rhetoric is only one of the tools which the opponent will use. Test his words; test his logic; test his facts. Make him state his arguments clearly. Do not be afraid to ask, "What exactly do you think that you mean by that?"

Once, at a friend's house, as I walked through the kitchen, his mother took occasion to lecture me on the meaning of the word "Vanity." To this day, I have no idea why this was on her mind, nor what she hoped to prove, nor what her argument meant to her. For that matter, I don't know why she chose me as the target of this argument.

"Did you know," she said, argumentatively, "That 'Vanity' means 'futility?' Doesn't that give a whole new meaning to the passage in Ecclesiastes, 'Vanity of vanities, says the preacher?' "

Well, that was impossible to argue, because first, I had no idea what she was on about, and secondly, because her fact – that Vanity means Futility – was correct. It can also mean pride, and can refer to a low counter or dresser with an attached mirror. I had never been under the illusion that Solomon was speaking of a particularly noteworthy dresser and mirror, so her argument, I'm afraid, was lost on me.

Had we been arguing as equals, I might have asked her, at this point, "And what precisely do you believe that that proves?" which would have clarified everything – provided, of course, that it was sufficiently clear in her mind that she could articulate it.

At any given point, you will probably find one of the following questions to be apropos, whether you ask the question of your opponent, or merely of yourself:

1.) Can you prove that? Is it really true?
2.) Is that truly relevant?
3.) What does that prove?
4.) Does that actually follow from what we know?

As it becomes clear that the opponent's argument is weak and flawed, you must begin your counter. You have parried his thrusts; now it is time for you to carry the battle to him.

Lay out your argument in the style that you've practiced. Start with your premises, connect the dots, and lead them to your conclusion. Some people try to use a style of Socratic Inquiry, which requires asking a series of questions. The problem is that a series of questions calls for a series of responses, and that may send the conversation in the wrong direction. I suggest not following the Socratic Method.

At this point style becomes important. The ideal argument is simple, elegant, clear, precise, and phrased in words of two syllables or less. A simple form would be:

"This is true. We know this because if that is true, then this must be true also. Here, we can clearly see that that is true. Thus, it follows that this is true."

As you can see, this argument simply builds on a syllogism, expanding it slightly into a more conversational style. The more conversational you can make it, without losing clarity, the more it improves. But be careful that you do not make your argument so conversational that you lose the sharp edge of your point.

In addition to arguing with atheists, I also sometimes argue politics. One of my friends and I noticed that many of our opponents followed a pattern: Deny the assertion, then admit the assertion and deny its significance, then admit the assertion and its significance, but claim that a counter-assertion renders it moot. In politics, this usually applies to an accusation: He didn't do that; He did it but it wasn't wrong; Okay, it was wrong but you guys have done worse.

You may hear this sort of argument used in apologetics, also. It is most likely to appear in the general category of Morals. If you see this sort of argument, the most effective way to deflate it is to challenge each step. Challenge the first assertion by showing that the person did the deed asserted. Challenge the second argument by showing why the deed is wrong. Say, "But that violates the principles that you espoused earlier."

You can also short-circuit the argument at the second step by saying, "That demonstrates my point: If your morals are not rooted in God, you can justify anything." This statement is a thrust aimed at the heart. It is a potential checkmate. Be prepared for an extreme and urgent defense – the atheist may go for denial, distraction, or retreat. Be prepared to drag them back on topic.

If they get to the third statement – That the person did the deed, and yes, it was wrong, but so what: Christians do bad stuff too – then the triad of moral equivalence is complete. First, permit yourself a smile, because you have just anticipated their every move, and they played into your hand. Then thank God for giving you the preparation and providence that you needed.

Now, examine the tools at your disposal. You can demand that they demonstrate that a Christian did a bad thing similar to the specified bad thing. This will lead you in a circle, back into the argument. You may find yourself debating whether Pol Pot was a choirboy, and whether his misdeeds were worse than Stalin's. It is a weaker tool, and will take a long time to bring results, but it can be effective.

Or you can seize the tool that was available at step two: Say, "That demonstrates my point. Morals not based in God are malleable." You may need to defend this thrust by showing that a misdeed by a Christian does not disprove Christianity – you've seen this before, and you are prepared for it.

I recommend the latter tool. It will be the more effective, and will help make your point. It's easy to lose your focus in an argument like this, but if you can keep your head, and realize what you're trying to say, you can bring the opponent to a dead stop.

Clarity of reasoning, and a clear goal, are sharp arrows in your quiver.

But there is a more excellent way, if you are bold, thinking clearly, and prepared for battle. You can take the philosophical path and raise the question of tertium quid. Tertium quid means "the third thing." You tell the opponent that clearly your moral and ethical system differs from his, because in your ethical system, the two described acts are very different.

Because of that, you need a third thing – a tertium quid – by which to measure the two ethical systems. To judge an ethical system, or to judge between two ethical systems, requires a higher ethical system than either one.

And with that, you now have a Dutch book: If the opponent denies that there exists a third thing, then he is tacitly admitting that his morals are merely meaningless preferences. The bad thing that he accuses the Christian of doing is not objectively bad; it is merely bad in his opinion because he denies the premise that God exists. He cannot accuse someone of being unethical, because without there being a higher standard – without God – his standard means as little as "I like ice cream."

If he allows reference to a "third thing," then he admits that morals are objective and thus are rooted in the nature of the universe – that is, the universe itself is moral, and in order to be moral, is necessarily an artifact of God. And God must exist in order to have an artifact. QED.

Okay, well, that's fine, Og, but what if it doesn't go so well?

Beware. If you let the opponent confuse you, and if you tighten your focus to believe that you must argue every assertion that your opponent makes, you will give him a chance to turn your argument backwards, and make you argue the opposite of your point. At that point, he can win by conceding.

If you start to lose focus, take a moment. Delay answering. Look at the original argument again, and refresh your mind. Give God a chance to whisper fresh thoughts into your mind. Then return and win. A good Bible verse for this situation is Micah 7:8, "Do not gloat over me, my enemy! Though I have fallen, I will rise. Though I sit in darkness, the LORD will be my light."

Do not allow confusion to overcome you. Fog and darkness are tools of the enemy. Let the LORD be your light. Renew your mind, and refresh your argument. Come back to the goal, and drive in to win. Remember the importance of a clear mind and a clear argument, focusing.

And this leads us to an important principle of apologetics: You cannot lose. You might lose an argument, but if so, you gain experience for the next round. You might lose your focus, but this will show you your weaknesses so that you can learn clarity. You might lose face, or lose pride, but you didn't need those anyway.

In Philippians 1:21, the Apostle Paul looked towards his upcoming trial, in which his life was at stake, and joyfully said, "To live is Christ, to die is gain." If Paul were released, he would go on declaring the gospel. To live was Christ, and Paul would win. And if Paul were condemned, and Nero took his life – which is what happened – then Paul would go to be with Christ in heaven. Again, Paul wins.

Live or die, Paul would win. And we have that same arrangement: If we lose the argument, we learn the enemy's argument and we learn to counter-attack. If we win the argument, we force the witnesses to evaluate the cause of Christ and open their minds to him. Either way, you win.

Have no fear. Keep your mind clear. Trust God. As our Lord repeatedly instructed Joshua, regarding the conquest of Canaan, "Be Strong and Courageous."

So, now what?

Okay, so you've read this book. Are you ready now to go out and wrestle atheists into logical conundrums, and chase the agnostics into the church?

Um, no. A book does not an apologist make. Maybe this is a step in the path – and may the Lord bless your journey. Or maybe this book has shown you that apologetics is not for you. Maybe it has been a bolster to your faith, or maybe it is here to remind you that you need further study.

There are many more books to read, and many more things to think about. A few additional books to read might be:

Lewis, C. S., *Screwtape Letters, The*, 1942, Macmillan, London
Lewis, C.S. *Great Divorce, The*, 1946, Macmillan, London
Lewis, C.S. *God in the Dock*, 1970, Eerdmans
Lewis, C.S. *Mere Christianity*, 1952, Macmillan, London
Lewis, C.S. *A Pilgrim's Regress*, 1933, Macmillan, London
Lewis, C.S. *The Abolition of Man*, 1943, Macmillan, London

Tozer, A.W. *Pursuit of God, The,* 1948, Christian Publications, Harrisburg, PA

Chesterton, G.K., *Everlasting Man, The,* 1925, Hodder & Stroughton, London

Little, Paul E., *Know What You Believe,* 1974, Inter-Varsity Press,

Sayers, Dorothy L. *Whimsical Christian, The,* 1978, Colliers

Plato, *Apologia,* Ca. 450 BC

God (by inspiration), *Bible, The,* 2000 BC – 90 AD

Durant, Will & Ariel, *Lessons of History, The,* 1968, Simon & Schuster, NYC

McDowell, Josh, *More Than a Carpenter,* 1977, Tyndale, Wheaton

McDowell, Josh, *Evidence That Demands a Verdict,* 1972, Here's Life, San Bernardino

CHAPTER FOURTEEN

Two Arguments That Are Like Atomic Bombs

THERE ARE TWO arguments that you can use which will leave atheists pulling their hair out. The arguments are unanswerable: In one case, the argument is clearly true but renders all other arguments useless; in the other case, the argument forces an intermediate conclusion that is extremely unpalatable to most people, and especially all atheists. The problem is that these are like atomic bombs: They leave the discussion in a wasted ruin from which no forward progress can be made.

Use these only with discretion and when it is truly important to win at any cost.

Induction and Deduction

All reasoning is either deduction – pasting together known facts to conclusively build larger facts, until we reach a final conclusion – or else induction, which is an assumption based upon observations.

For example, suppose that we deduce that tomorrow's picnic will be brightly lit. We deduce that the weather will be clear, and that the sun will be shining. We base these deductions, at their roots, on observations – that the sun rises every day; that clear summer days are likely to be bright and hot.

But these observations are not conclusive; and the deductions that we draw from them are not necessarily reliable. The fact that the sun has risen every morning of our lives does not necessarily mean that the sun will rise tomorrow.

A famous mathematician, Bertrand Russell, once gave the example of a chicken which noted that, every night, the farmer selected one of the other chickens and killed it to eat as his dinner. From this, the chicken might draw the inductive conclusion that the farmer will always, without exception, choose one of the other chickens. She would thus falsely believe herself safe.

If there is no observation and induction, then there can be no deduction. And lacking deduction, there can be no proof, ever. Since induction is not provable, but is necessary for deductions, nothing can be proven, if we do not draw conclusions based purely on assumptions. There is no proof that any effect truly resulted from a cause.

This is the great induction/deduction problem. Even the scientific method, which deductively tests hypotheses, first inductively creates those hypotheses. So here's the argument:

Nothing can actually be proven deductively, because deduction rests upon induction, which is inherently fallible. Therefore nothing can be proven. For further reading on this, see the writings of David Hume, an eighteenth century English Philosopher.

There it is. It's indisputable. It's arguable, and folks will argue about it if you give them a chance, but it can't be refuted. It also renders it impossible for you to prove your own case as well, so it does tend to produce a stalemate. If you find yourself having used this argument, and you need a way to get back from the brink, here's a way home:

Og's Principle of Induction (yes, I made it up) states that, "As experience increases, the reliability of assumptions based on observation approaches one-hundred percent." In other words, as we see the sun rise each day, without fail, the reliability of our assumption (that it will always rise) increases, until we can say it with almost perfect reliability.

So there you are: The Poison Argument, and its antidote. But wait, there's more.

Proof of the Existence of God

Yes, yes, I know. The ancient proofs of the existence of God, such as the Ontological argument, the Cosmological argument, etc., have all been shown to be faulty in some way. Some people even argue that it is impossible to prove the existence of God. One atheist mathematician based his arguments against God, in part, on the fallibility of the ancient proofs of God (even though, logically, that just means that they are weak arguments, not that they are therefore wrong).

But on the other hand, we Christians know that God is real. We have felt the power of His hand in our life. We may even have heard Him give us a Holy Nudge, or He may even have spoken to us. So we have subjective, internal, unrepeatable proof. We just don't have objective repeatable proof that we can show to others.

Aside from this proof, of course.

We begin three hundred years ago, with a man named George Berkeley. In 1710, he wrote a Treatise (which you can read if you're interested) in which he argued that the universe was not objective.

Here's what's at stake: If the universe is objective, then it always behaves the same way. It is consistent and immutable: Pi will always equal 3.1415926535897932384626... as opposed to equaling 22/7 today and exactly 3 tomorrow. But if the universe is subjective, then the universe depends on being observed – to be is to be observed, as Berkeley argued.*

Berkeley based his argument on the fact that all of our information about the universe consists of perceptions. That is, we see a tree, which means that our brain has had an idea, and that idea is: "My eyes tell me that there is a tree."

Every perception – touch, sound, taste, sight – is nothing but an idea. For all we know, we may just be brains in tanks, with wires that tell us the things we think we know. Yes, several Hollywood movies have been made on this topic. Berkeley argues that there cannot exist a "naked thought" – that is, a thought without a brain around it – and therefore there cannot be a naked perception – a sight without an eye that sees it, and conveys it to a brain that thinks it. Therefore, says Berkeley, the universe is subjective.

As an aside at this point: Berkeley provides us an either/or argument – a double-barreled cinch – in our argument. If Berkeley was wrong, and a thing can exist without being perceptible, then it is not unreasonable to believe in an invisible God. If Berkeley was right, then God necessarily exists. Either way, Berkeley provides a starting point for us, but as we shall see, Berkeley was absolutely right.

So how do we know Berkeley was right?

A fellow named Samuel Johnson tried to refute Berkeley by kicking a stone. But that doesn't prove that Berkeley was wrong: In Berkeley's opinion, Johnson thought that he perceived resistance when he thought that he swung his foot towards what he thought was a stone. Immanuel Kant, a German philosopher, also presented a very good argument about what we can know and what we cannot know.

Kant's arguments, however, explain why we think that the universe might not be objective, but they don't prove that it is objective. Causing us to doubt our argument is not proof against our argument. Ridicule is not refutation.

So what else may tell us whether or not the universe is objective?

Well, remember when we said that in an objective universe, the rules are always the same? That pi is always a constant, and that the laws of the universe are always the same? Well, it turns out that under certain circumstances, the rules of the universe change… and don't make much sense.

A fellow by the name of Erwin Schrodinger demonstrated this when he tried to mock three of his rivals at the same time. He made up a "thought experiment," which was his way of mocking Albert Einstein's thought experiments. The specific thought experiment was intended to mock Werner Heisenberg and Neils Bohr, whose quantum mechanics equations – called "the Copenhagen Interpretation" – made for some ridiculous conclusions.

The thought experiment goes like this:

Suppose that there is a cat in a box. The box is closed, and we can't tell from outside whether the cat inside is alive or dead. We can't hear it, see, it, or feel it move. There is also a "diabolical device" inside the box, so that when a certain atom decays, the device will kill the cat.

Obviously, we don't know if the cat is alive or dead, and the only way to find out is to open the box. Well, this is where it gets weird: According to the Copenhagen Interpretation, the cat is BOTH alive and dead at the same time.

Wait, you say. How can a cat be BOTH alive AND dead? Well, in an objective universe, it cannot be: It must be one or the other. And yet the math is inescapable: It is both.

Don't make a mistake here: Some atheists have argued against this argument on the grounds that not knowing whether the cat is alive or dead does not prove that the universe is subjective. But they have missed the critical point: Quantum Mechanics tells us that we DO know the state of the cat, and that the state of the cat is BOTH.

This is not an argument from silence, which would have the form: "We don't know whether the cat is alive or dead, and therefore the universe is subjective" (what a silly argument that would be!). Instead we are saying that we DO know the state of the cat, and that state is simply too weird to be true in an objective universe, and therefore the universe is not objective.

Well, suppose that we don't know what to think of Schrodinger's Cat, and we aren't ready to accept Berkeley's "Naked Thought" argument. How else might we know if the universe is objective?

As it turns out, there's more.

Quantum Tunneling is another simply impossible phenomenon in an objective universe. It essentially calls for electrons to be able to pass through an impassible barrier based solely on the fact that there is a "non-zero" probability of the electrons being there.

To put this into perspective: There is a non-zero probability of me waking up in Toledo, Ohio. This probability is linked to the non-zero probability of me getting onto an airplane and flying to Toledo, so that I can go to sleep there. If I rule out going to sleep in Toledo, the probability of me waking up there is exactly zero. I am also ignoring the possibility of me passing out at a bachelor party and being loaded onto a Toledo-bound bus by drunken friends (thanks, Cameron).

But if I were an electron, and there were a non-zero probability of me waking up in Toledo, then sometimes I would wake up in Toledo without having gone to sleep there the night before. And that's not possible in an objective universe.

But it happens. Every silicon chip on the planet works on Quantum Tunneling. An impossible thing happens routinely when you boot your computer. Is that possible in an objective universe? I think not.

As an aside here: I once presented this theory to an astrophysicist with whom I am vaguely acquainted, and he was kind enough to comment. He objected on philosophical grounds to my use of physics, even theoretically, to prove God – even though he is a Christian, he felt that it was an affront to his profession. He also denied Berkeley's conclusion, repeating Johnson's kicking-of-the-rock. But he was not able to show that I was mis-stating either the Schrodinger's Cat problem, or the theoretical aspects of Quantum Tunneling.

I am indebted to him for his input, even though he was resistant to considering the idea at all, and I promised him that I would not associate his name with his comments. I have kept that promise.

Returning to our point: Clearly, then, the universe is subjective. But are we completely certain? Well, as it turns out – there's more.

Quantum Entanglement is another non-objective phenomenon. To explain Quantum Entanglement in a few words is not easy. One way to imagine it would be to think of two guys who work in a convenience store, on opposite shifts. When Al is in, Ben is out; when Ben is in, Al is out. They pass in the doorway every twelve hours, as regularly as clockwork.

In Quantum Mechanics terms, we would say that Al and Ben are entangled, by which we mean that if we know the state of one – at work or off work – we know the state of the other, and that it is the opposite of the first. I must disclaim here: To our knowledge, Quantum Entanglement only occurs in subatomic particles, and never in humans. Al and Ben are merely illustrating the concept for us.

Now, suppose that Al quits and goes to work at an all night gas station. He now works opposite, say, Chuck; and Ben now works opposite, perhaps, Dan. We would rightly expect Al and Chuck to be entangled, and for Ben and Dan to be entangled.

But here the plot thickens. According to Quantum Mechanics – again, we are examining phenomena in the larger world which actually happen in the extremely miniscule world, at subatomic levels – According to QM, Al and Ben remain entangled.

If, for example, Ben continued to work the night shift, then Al, at his unrelated new job, would necessarily work the day shift. If Al were to call in sick at the gas station, Ben would work an extra shift at the convenience store, even though there would no longer be a logical reason for this to happen.

For many people, Quantum Entanglement – because it tells us that particles which used to be related remain related even when the relationship ends – is a bridge too far. It would be easy, at this point, to say that this shows a flaw in the mathematics of Quantum Mechanics. This incredulity would be understandable, or even acceptable, were it not for one problem: there has been experimental confirmation of Quantum Entanglement.

An experiment with a sodium-plasma laser showed that the output beam escaped the far side of the chamber in a faster time than the speed of light would permit. This would only be possible if the sodium atoms receiving the excitement, at one end of the chamber, were quantum entangled with atoms which changed energy states at the other end of the chamber, resulting in the laser beam output.

So we are faced with yet another example of a circumstance too strange to occur in an objective universe. This means that the universe is not objective.

To recap, four things tell us that the universe is not objective:

1.) As Berkeley assures us, there cannot exist a "**Naked Thought**."
2.) **The Dual-Wave** of the Copenhagen Interpretation shows a non-objective phenomenon (the cat is both alive and dead).

3.) **Quantum Tunneling** is another objectively impossible, but real, phenomenon (and that's why your computer works).

4.) **Quantum Entanglement** is the strangest of all of these objectively impossible (but real) phenomena.

As an aside, I once had an atheist to whom I presented this argument attempt to refute it on the grounds that there are "explanations" for quantum phenomena. He ignored Berkeley, Tunneling, and Entanglement, and pointed out that the "Many Worlds" theory is an explanation of Schrodinger's Cat.

The problem is that this atheist had apparently gone to the nearest online encyclopedia and looked up "Answers to Schrodinger's Cat," without attempting to understand the problem or the answers. The Many Worlds theory explains only one part of the problem, namely, why the cat's state becomes fixed when you open the box and see the cat with your own eyes.

The Many Worlds theory maintains that the observer becomes "entangled" with one of the two states of the cat, and that there is a parallel universe in which another observer opened the box and became entangled with the opposite state of the cat.

This is leaping from the frying pan into the fire. In order to maintain a belief in a universe that is objective, the atheist embraced a theory that calls for phenomena that would make it subjective, namely entanglement, and an infinite number of parallel universes (at least one pair of universes for every possible atomic decay, it would seem). To keep the universe making sense to him, he made the universe ridiculous.

It pays to read carefully, and to understand the theories. Atheists love to bluff, and in this case calling the bluff was quite entertaining. But returning to the naked thought, the cat in the box, tunneling, and entanglement; these four clues make the conclusion obvious: The universe is not objective. We have proven it.

But that was not our goal: we set out to prove the existence of God. So fasten your mental seatbelts, here we go:

Berkeley, back in 1710, argued that although we know the universe is not objective – it is clearly subjective, and the existence of any object depends upon that object being perceived, as we have shown – we are faced with the difficulty that the universe appears to be objective.

When we place an object in a drawer, we cease to observe it. We may even forget that it is there, or we may leave an object in a drawer that another person will be surprised to discover. The object in the drawer persists – that is, it continues to exist.

If to be requires that a thing be observed, and no human can observe it, it must be observed by someone who is not human: The Omniscient Super-observer. Further, consider the other things that exist: pi, natural logarithms, Pascal's law, Planck's constant. None of these are tangible or perceptible, and yet they remain true and constant. Clearly, they too are observed, and thus we know that the Super-observer is intelligent and sentient.

Emotions persist, and individuality. Thus we know that the Super-observer is personal and has emotions. Infinity exists, and thus we know that the Super-observer is infinite.

We have a name for a personal, infinite, omniscient Super-observing Being. We call him God. By His perception, the Worlds formed – "And He is before all things, and in Him all things consist," as Paul tells us in Colossians 1:17. Creator God; Omniscient Personal Infinite One; He must logically exist.

I once dragged an atheist this far, and made him face the idea of an omniscient super-observer. His response was merely that even if my logic were correct (and he could find no holes in it), this Omniscient Superobserver still might not be the YHWH, Creator-God and Father of Jesus Christ, the Triune God of Christianity.

No, we have not proven that The God is Our God. That will come later. For now, it is enough to have proven that there exists exactly one God. Squirm though you might, it is clearly a fact, beyond denial, that there exists One God.

There you have them, as promised: Two arguments which are like Nuclear bombs. One destroys reason; the other destroys the objectivity of the universe. Use them with care.

CONCLUSION

So, Og, who are you, anyway?

A FAIR QUESTION. When someone writes a book with so authoritative a tone as this, it is safe to assume that the writer is some sort of an expert, or at least believes that he is. So who's this Og fellow, anyway?

"Og" is just a guy, an ordinary caveman, with no special education or skills or qualifications; that's who I am. I'm not a particularly holy person; I am a sinner saved by grace and a recovering sin addict. I sin daily and must keep asking for Christ's forgiveness.

I've read a lot. I could list the books, but you'll find many of them in this book, anyway. I'm a smart guy. I've got a better than average IQ, and I've tried to use it well, for the edification of the church. I'm a Christian, and specifically a Southern Baptist. I have a strong faith, in a powerful religious belief that has literally changed the world.

And none of these make me an expert.

This book hopefully speaks for itself. Everything in this book until now can be found elsewhere; I hope that I have stated those facts, details and methods more clearly, perhaps, or at least with more flair than in some stodgy textbook.

But that doesn't answer the question: what is an average-guy caveman Christian doing writing a book? What's my motivation? Well, I believe that the Lord gives talents to the church, and that we are obligated to use those talents for the building-up – the edification – of the church. I look around me today, and I see a lot of confusion about basic Christian truths and basic logic. I am amazed at how many Christians believe that their faith is illogical, or that Science cannot be reconciled with their faith.

That grieves me. I know that the Bible is true, because I know that God is alive. I know that God is alive because I have seen His hand in my life, and I have heard what I believe to be His voice.

To start at the beginning: I was raised in a Christian home.

My mother attended church at the Southern Baptist church that happened to be on our street. She began going to church when my oldest siblings were small, because she thought that they needed to be exposed to church, but she soon realized that the messages were speaking to her. She came to put her faith in Jesus Christ as her Personal Savior.

By the time I appeared on the scene, my mother was very active in the church. My father, while he chose not to attend himself, had no objections to having her take us kids to church. Eventually, however, the gospel affected Him also. He became friends with the pastor of the church, and this eventually led to my father also making a profession of faith in Christ, when I was about seven. It was not a merely outward appearance; he became as active in church as my mother was, and soon he was teaching Sunday School classes.

Just before I turned nine, I began to feel a drawing towards God in my own heart. At the conclusion of a Baptist service, there is a final song called an "Invitation." It is an opportunity for those to whom God has spoken, during the service, to respond to Him. Whenever we would sing the invitation song, I would feel a pull towards the front, as if there were an invisible string through my heart tugging me towards the pastor.

I already knew the "Roman Road" to Salvation, as the Sunday School teachers called it: Romans 3:23, Romans 6:23, Romans 5:8, Romans 10:9-10. I knew that I was a sinner, even though I'd never robbed a bank or committed a murder: All have sinned, and fall short of the glory of God. I knew that Jesus Christ had died for the sins of mankind. I knew that I needed to receive Jesus Christ as my personal Savior and Lord, inviting Him to become an active part of my young life.

But I resisted those tugs. I still don't know why. One Sunday I found myself in the outside aisle, being drawn towards the front; my feet, as if of their own will, were walking towards the altar. I panicked. I felt that I couldn't turn around and go back; it would look strange. People had seen me in the aisle. But what would I say to the pastor? What was I supposed to do?

Sometimes people would go to the front and kneel at the altar to pray during the invitation. It was a simple wooden frame covered in faux leather. There was nothing secret or sacred to it, in and of itself, but it was designed to allow one to kneel and do business with God.

To this point, I had sat through many services, Vacation Bible Schools, children's programs, and other church events. I had never encountered anything mystically spiritual there. I had no reason to expect anything unusual this time, either. So I hit upon a simple plan: I would kneel for a moment at the altar, say a short prayer, and before the last chorus of the invitation, walk back to my seat. No one would think anything unusual about it. Simple.

But as I knelt, I became aware of the immediate presence of Almighty God. I didn't see a vision or hear voices, but I felt God's presence. It was as if I were kneeling before His throne, with His full attention focussed on me. If I could put the feeling into words, the words would be, "Are you through fooling around?"

I knew then that I was not supposed to have knelt down for a sham of a prayer. I was supposed to have gone to the pastor, and explained my need for Jesus Christ. God had made an appointment with me that day, and had drawn me to Himself.

I said the briefest prayer I've ever prayed – three words – and returned to my seat as quickly as propriety would allow. One of my brother's friends asked me about it later. "Why did you even go up there? You barely even knelt, and just got right back up." I had no answer. I couldn't explain what had happened.

About a week later, I responded to an invitation, willingly giving in to that tugging. I prayed a brief prayer – not as brief as the other, of course – in which I admitted that I was a sinner, asked Jesus to forgive me, and acknowledged that He died for my sins. I asked him to enter my life and make me at one with God.

I'd love to tell you that from then on, I've lived a perfect life for God. The problem is that I'd be lying. I did try to live a Christian life, but as I entered high school, I felt that I had to protect my "fragile" faith from "science," because I thought that science would "disprove all that stuff."

After high school, I joined the Navy. This was a moral trial, to say the least. Sailors are known for language and practices inconsistent with the Christian life. I confess that I indulged in some of these practices, and not in others. This led me into a moral crisis that made my earlier crisis of faith more emphatic. I no longer practiced my beliefs, and I had doubts about whether I could reconcile them with science.

You may ask how I could ignore my prior experience with God. I simply convinced myself that that was a childish emotional moment, and a figment of my imagination. The human mind, when not governed by Logic, has a marvelous capacity for denial.

I began to slip from my morality. I started to go places and to do things that I knew were not consistent with Christian practice. I made immoral friends. I did immoral things. And the result – well, as the scripture says, "Whatsoever a man shall sow, that shall he also reap." The good things in my life began to unravel.

One afternoon, listening to the radio, feeling dejected and alone, I heard the DJ say that the next song was intended as a "dedication." For young readers: That meant that someone had called the station and asked that the particular song be played as a message or reminder to someone else. An idea entered my mind, as strange as it seemed, that the song was meant for me, so I listened intently to hear what song would be played. It was an old Gospel song, reassuring the listener that God sent His love on Dove's wings.

My heart broke with the first notes, and I wept openly. As much as I had messed things up, God was telling me, specifically, that He loved me. His hand was still on me. As David said in Psalm 139, "Though I make my bed in Hell, behold: Thou art with me." It was true: Even in that dark hour, God was there. I wasn't ready to return to Him, but He was still calling to me.

I reformed my morals and tried to find a comfortable balance between being absolutely Godly, which I thought would make me a target for jokes among my peers, and being a slave to my flesh, which would have repelled the more moral of those whom I knew. There is no such balance, of course. It can't be done. Still, in an effort to avoid facing God, I began to try to rationalize the things that I was doing. I tried to make my spiritual battle into an intellectual matter. Ah, but God is the King of the intellect as well.

Curiously, the phrase that kept coming to mind was a Biblical question: "Why halt ye between two opinions?" I eventually resolved to settle the matter once and for all: I would test my beliefs against the real world, and let the chips fall where they may. If I discovered that my beliefs were not true, then I resolved to reject them and live in a godless world; If my beliefs were true, then I would live as a Christian and rededicate my life to my God. It was a frightening moment: I was either about to abandon my upbringing, or to commit to do whatever God wanted.

I began to study and read about whether or not God existed. All of the atheist writings that I found were straw men. They built a false concept of God, and then tried to tear Him down based on that misconception.

One writer pointed to the fact that Jesus once cursed a fig tree, and based upon that, declared that Jesus was not the best and wisest of men, with the implied argument that therefore He was not divine. It was a chain of misconceptions jumping to a non sequitur conclusion.

On the other hand, reading C. S. Lewis caused me to see that belief in God is logical, and not in conflict with science. Reading about his conflicts, and the long philosophical road that had brought him home to "Mother Kirk" – that sealed my decision.

I found a quiet place and knelt there, submitting my life to God and asking God to restore me to His service. I cannot describe the overwhelming joy that came with this decision. It was just like the parable of the prodigal son: God ran to meet me. Where I had dreaded giving up my moral freedom, I found that the things I lost did nothing good for me, and I was amazed at what I gained. I began to find scripture passages that left me amazed. I felt God's grace.

Where my earlier moral failures, mild though they were, tended to repel my friends, my renewed moral stance drew me into fellowship with new friends. Even those people in my life who were not moral and who did not believe began to develop a respect for my beliefs, and made an effort not to offend them.

During my "prodigal" period, I could not find a purpose in life. I read many existential philosophers, and found that life not invested in God is pointless; but in God I found that my life had purpose, and a plan, and a structure imposed from without.

God has used me to affect the lives of others. God has allowed me to be a small part of the process of drawing people to Himself. I've been active in the church, helping to strengthen it. I've served silently and gladly to make the ministries of other Christians stronger.

I say this not to boast – I've even used a pseudonym here so that the glory will belong to God alone – but rather to show how God has overcome my selfish immorality and helped me to deny myself, following Him. I'm not perfect by any means. I sin daily, and sometimes hourly. But God is good, and His Grace covers me. I am still addicted to sin, but I'm on the road to recovery.

In looking back now, I am grateful to God that He drew me back to Himself. The things I laid aside – immoral words and deeds – were worth nothing to me, and could not make me happy. But Christ can make me happy, and to serve Him is the fulfillment and purpose that life calls for.

I've been irreverent in this book, and even flippant. I've been arrogant, and I've been dismissive of ideas that contradict what I believe. Let me now be perfectly serious, and as solemn as I am capable of being: I hope and pray that this book will lead someone, perhaps some several people, to look up and ask God if perhaps He really is there. I must leave the success of this effort, if there is any, to the Holy Spirit. But, Friend, I urge you, in all sincerity, from the depths of my soul, to pray right now that God will show Himself to you. What do you have to lose?

GLOSSARY

THESE ARE THE meaning of words and phrases as they are used in this book. You may find different meanings expressed in other Lexicons, but this is how these words and phrases are used in this book.

Absurd – Contrary to logic; leading to a contradiction or an obvious error; not capable of being reconciled to the known facts.

Aesthetics – That branch of Philosophy that concerns itself with the study of beauty in sound, appearance, and concepts. When an idea is "Elegant" the idea is aesthetically pleasing in addition to any virtues that it may have in its logic.

Allege, Alleged, Allegation – (To state) Something which is as yet unproven; The alleged robber.

Assert, Assertion – (To make) A firm declaration which is not yet proven. "But whom Paul asserts to be alive." Acts 26:19

Ambiguous – Indefinite, not clearly defined, not distinct, vague, meaning more than one thing.

Ambiguous Definition – A word or phrase used to mean more than one thing, or an ill-defined word or phrase.

Antecedent – That which goes before, or the first clause of a general premise.

Apochrypha – Literally, "the hidden." In theology, the section of the Bible that lies between the Old and New Testaments, and that Protestant and Non-conformist Christians do not accept as canonical.

Apologetics – From the Greek word Apologia, meaning defense, Apologetics is the verbal defense of an idea or argument. In Ancient Greece, an apologia was a defense presented in court when one was accused of a crime. Christian apologetics is the defense of the Christian faith.

Apologia – A dialog of Plato in which Socrates defends himself against charges of impiety, corrupting the young, and causing false things to appear true. Considered Socrates' best work.

Arbitrary – An attribute of something which can be replaced with something similar. Opposite of Intrinsic. The engine of a car is intrinsic, but the hub caps are arbitrary.

Argument – Either a verbal dispute, or a line of reasoning; *There was an argument over the menu,* or *His argument seems logical.*

Argument by Desire – A proof offered by C. S. Lewis to the effect that just as a human's thirst implies that he is a creature that naturally drinks water, so our desire for the Divine is evidence that we were made for fellowship with God.

Aristotle – A philosopher who developed the logical syllogism. Aristotle also established a system of science and biological nomenclature. Aristotle's system of science was used until Newton's system of Kinematics (also called Newtonian Physics, or Newton's Laws of Motion) was developed in the late 18th century. A student of Plato.

Arminianism – the belief that salvation comes by a Free Will choice.

Assumption – Something that a person assumes, and uses as a foundation for an argument. This may also be a postulate or an axiom. Some assumptions are not clearly stated in an argument, and may not be obvious to the reader.

Atonement – To reconcile by correcting an offense; to bring together; to make two people "At One" or as one. Jesus' act of Atonement sets us at one with God.

Attribute – Something which describes something else. A blue car has the attribute of being blue. And the attribute of being a car.

A. W. Tozer – Christian theologian; author of *The Pursuit of God*.

Begging the Question – An error related to a circular argument. When one jumps to a conclusion without having gone through the logical steps, one may be said to be begging the question. For example, "Let's give this man a fair trial and then we'll hang him" assumes that the trial will result in a guilty verdict, despite the guilt not being proven yet. It begs the question of guilt, since the suggested hanging assumes the accused to be guilty. Many people misuse it to mean, "That begs FOR the [clarifying] question:" which is not the correct meaning of the phrase.

Calvinism – The belief that salvation is predestined.

Canon, Canonical – Canon is the accepted center or approved core of a set of writings. The Biblical Canon is the Bible itself. While most Christians acknowledge the 66 books of the Bible as canon, Catholics and Episcopalians also accept a small set of writings written between 400 BC and 1 AD, collectively called the "Apochrypha."

Circular Argument: Related to "Begging the question," a Circular Argument uses the desired conclusion as one of the premises.

Cognitive Biases – A form of fallacy that results from intellectual illusions. If, for example, we tend to summarize data based on the outcome that we desire to see, rather than actually analyzing the data properly, we are engaged in a cognitive bias, which prevents us from realizing the objective facts.

Cognitive Dissonance – A form of mental failing that occurs when the brain is confused by repetition or isolation. Cults have used cognitive dissonance by isolating prospective converts from outside contact, and then repeating key phrases or mantras until the convert's mind begins to detach the meanings of those phrases. A mild example of cognitive dissonance is found in the motto of propaganda artists: "Repeat a lie often enough and it becomes the truth."

Conclusion – The last line of an argument, often starting with the word "Therefore" or the word "Thus." Sometimes "Thus" is the Latin Ergo. In a syllogism, the conclusion follows from the General premise and the Specific premise.

Consequences – The natural results – usually bad – of an action. The consequences of sin are death and hell.

Consequent – That which comes after, or the second clause of a general premise (see syllogisms).

Contradiction – Literally, "Speaking Against." A contradiction can be a dispute on a matter of fact, or can be a logical absurdity (in which the conclusion "contradicts" a known fact). Two stories that don't match are "contradictory." A contradiction can often be an indication of the invalidity of an argument.

C.S. Lewis – Clive Staples "Jack" Lewis, b. 1898, d. 1963; Cambridge Professor, author of *The Screwtape Letters, Mere Christianity, God in the Dock, A Pilgrim's Regress, the Abolition of Man, The Great Divorce,* and many other books. Although not Lewis' primary field of study, he is best known for his theological works, all of which are excellent for apologetic studies.

Deconstruct – to break down the elements of a concept or style, usually by constructing an ironic version of the concept or style. For example, we might say that the movie "Unforgiven" deconstructs the classic Western novel or movie by making a movie in which the elements of Western movies are exposed and questioned.

Deduction – A conclusion based upon known facts, applied to each other in order to bridge an area of ignorance. Any syllogism is a deductive argument. It is important to realize, however, that every deductive argument is based, at its most basic point, upon an inductive argument.

Definitive – Complete, defining, and without need for discussion.

Denomination – one of many divisions of Christianity, most of which agree in most of their beliefs. Roman Catholicism, the Southern Baptist Convention, and Methodism are all denominations.

Dichotomy – Cutting in two, or splitting an idea into two competing possibilities.

Discernment – The ability to notice differences in the thoughts and intents of people, or to judge good and evil. Discernment may be simple wisdom, or may be a spiritual gift. It may be manifested in logic and argument, or as a word of knowledge or wisdom.

Discipline – The process of studying, or of being a disciple; to undergo a course of study; the course of study itself.

Double-barreled Cinch – A win-win argument. It works by presenting a choice from which either response leads to the conclusion you are attempting to demonstrate.

Dutch Book – A wager that cannot be lost. When Paul states that "*To live is Christ, to die is gain*," he is creating a "Dutch book" because there is no possible circumstance in which he does not win.

Edify, Edification – Edify means "to build up." An edifice is a building. Edification means the process of building up, especially building the mind or spirit of a person or persons, as, "For the edification of the church."

Entities – Things or beings.

Epistemology – That branch of Philosophy which concerns itself with those things that can or can not be known. One might consider a poker game as an exercise in applied Epistemology.

Essential – Pertaining to the essence of something. Or, a part of the essence of, and thus crucial to, something.

Ethics – That branch of Philosophy which is dedicated to how a person should behave. In Classical times, ethics concerned issues of "piety" (reverence to one's god or family). Today, ethics concerns morality.

Etymology – The way that a word developed; the roots from which the word was formed. This often gives insight into the word itself, and what it means.

Euthyphro, Euthyphro Dilemma – In the Socrates dialog of the same name, Socrates asks Euthyphro whether piety consists of doing what the gods approve of, or whether the gods approve of actions because they are pious. When used by modern atheists, they usually mean to ask whether one believes that God is Good, or that good is a property of (and thus a higher standard than) God. In this case, "Good" (Goodness, Morality) is substituted for piety (the classical guide to behavior). To answer this dilemma, realize that our understanding of God is imperfect and flawed. We cannot see God as He knows Himself to be. Thus, when we say that God is good, we are in fact saying that he exemplifies those attributes which He has taught us to value. See chapter six for details.

Everlasting Man, the – A book by G.K. Chesterton, exploring two main premises: That mankind is unique among the animals, and that Jesus of Nazareth was unique among men. Chesterton also points out most atheists today are not truly outside the church, but are merely spoiled Christians, who must either draw closer to, or move farther from the church, in order to judge her objectively.

Excluded Middle – When there is a small set of possible answers to a question (usually two) and the answer cannot be "Both" nor "Neither" then we have excluded the middle. The question "Are you alive?" can only be answered "Yes" or "no." It cannot be answered "Both" nor "neither" (quantum mechanics notwithstanding) and thus the "middle" is "excluded."

Exegesis – The process of drawing out a meaning from a text. We must always be careful to use proper rules when drawing out a meaning, so that we do not insert a meaning into the text.

Existential, existentialism – A certain philosophical position which assumes that God does not exist. Existentialism shaped much of intellectual thought after World War 2. While there are not a set of defining beliefs to Existentialism, there are certain lines of thought which can be called Existential. For example, a belief that everything is futile would most likely be an existential thought. The idea that justice cannot be obtained is an existential thought. Also, any story in which a man awakens to discover that he is a cockroach is definitely an existential story.

Fallacy – an argument that seems logical, but is based on poor assumptions and bad logic.

False Dichotomy – An argument based on there being two, and only two, possible choices, when, in fact, more choices exist. For example, "Did you have eggs or bacon for breakfast?" is a false dichotomy: You might have had "both" or "neither." See also "Excluded Middle" and "Unexcluded Middle."

Filial Piety – Respect and Reverence for, and one's duties towards, one's family, and especially one's parents. Friendship may also be considered a form of filial piety (a friend as a figurative brother).

Follow, Follow Logically – To be the logical conclusion which is required from a General Premise and a Specific Premise. To complete a logical argument. The conclusion that makes sense, based on the premises, "follows" from them.

Formal Fallacies – Logic errors which come from a bad syllogism: Denying the antecedent, Affirming the consequent, or Ambiguous Definitions.

G. K. Chesterton – Early 20th century writer; author of "The Everlasting Man," a book that strongly argues in support of the Christian Faith. If you can find it, read it.

Gameliel – A famous rabbi of the first century BC / First century AD; a teacher of Saul of Tarsus, who was later called Paul the Apostle.

General Premise – In a syllogism, the first premise is called the general premise, and usually has the form, "If A, then B."

Gnostic – Gnostic means, "Pertaining to knowledge," and refers to an intellectual movement during the first and second centuries. Gnostics – call them "Know it alls" – believed that they had a secret knowledge which imparted Salvation. They believed that only through knowing secret things could a person be saved. They were intellectual snobs, and held beliefs that were not Christian teachings. Some Gnostics taught that the secret knowledge necessary for salvation was sexual in natures, and expressed this belief through orgies and perverse practices. Gnostic writings, no matter what you may see in television specials, were never a part of Christian Canon.

Grace – Grace is something that we receive but do not deserve. God gives us His Grace by giving us the gift of eternal life with Him (Romans 6:23). We don't deserve it. He graciously gives it anyway.

Heliocentricity, Heliocentric – The belief that the earth revolves around the sun, as opposed to the belief that the sun revolves around the earth, as our casual observations would otherwise suggest. Literally, "Sun-center-ism."

Hermeneutics – The set of rules by which we draw a meaning out of a text. See also Exegesis.

Hypothesis – An "Educated Guess" based on information gathered. By forming and testing hypotheses, one is able to eliminate false ideas, and thus narrow down to correct ideas.

Ichthys, "**IXOYE**" – A Greek acronym for the Greek words that mean "Jesus Christ, God's Son, Savior." The word "Ichthys" is

Greek for "Fish," so you may see the word associated with a crude sketch of a fish.

Improper Question – A question which makes contradictory assumptions, such as "Could God make a rock so large He couldn't lift it?" which assumes first, that God is omnipotent, and second, that He is not. A logically improper question cannot be answered because it contradicts itself. The question is not improper in the sense of being rude, but improper as an improper fraction is improper.

Induction – A conclusion based on observations, along with an assumption that those observations demonstrate a reliable pattern. To assert that the sun will rise tomorrow, based upon our lifetime of observations, is an inductive argument. (see Deduction).

Informal Fallacies – Fallacies which result from bad logic, but which are not a formal fallacy. Examples of informal fallacies are "false dichotomies" and "appeal to the emotions."

Iniquity – One of two categories of sin mentioned in the Bible. Iniquity is to "miss the mark" or to fall short of a goal. See also, transgression.

Intangible – Not able to be touched. Love, happiness, thoughts, and the human soul are all intangible.

Intrinsic – An important central core attribute of something. Jesus' sacrifice was intrinsic to his mission.

Invitation, Altar Call – A part of an evangelical worship service in which congregants are invited to come to the altar and make decisions, such as a profession of faith, or to join the church. One may also come to the altar to pray, or to request prayer by the pastor.

Irrelevant – Not related to the topic at hand, immaterial, not pertinent, beside the point, moot.

Irreverant – Not respectful. God deserves our reverence; Sophists and most so-called Philosophers do not.

Jesus of Nazareth, Jesus Christ, Jesus the Messiah – An historical man who lived from about 1 BC to about 33 AD. He worked miracles, and called Himself the Messiah (see John 4:26, for example). Messiah, or "anointed one," was the name used by the Jews for a divine King who was to come, based on ancient prophecies (compare, for example, Psalm 22 (circa 1000 BC) and Isaiah 53 (circa 500 BC) with the crucifixion of Christ in the gospels). Christ is the Latin word meaning "Anointed," and is usually applied to Jesus, as a title. Jesus died for the sins of mankind and rose again on the third day.

John – Two men of this name appear significantly in the life of Christ: John the Baptist (second cousin of Jesus; his mother Elisabeth was Mary's cousin) and John the Disciple, who wrote the New Testament books of John (also called the Gospel of John), 1 John, 2 John, 3 John (letters), and the Revelation of John (also called Revelation). John the Disciple was the second most prolific of New Testament writers. Bible novices sometimes confuse John the Baptist with John the Disciple.

Justified – Made just, or reconciled with Justice. My sin is justified by Jesus' sacrifice, and it is "Just-if-I'd" never sinned (Okay, that should be "Just-as-if-I'd," but that doesn't fit the pun).

Law of Grace – In Paul's letter to the Romans, he talks about how the moral laws outlined in the Old Testament were mainly intended to show us that we were not capable of being moral; All have sinned and fall short of the glory of God. Paul then shows us a better way to live, having been forgiven by Christ: The Law of Grace, which is to say, obedience to God based not on fear of punishment or the following of obscure rules for those rules' own sake, but on our love for Christ, who loved us first. A powerful love, such as the redeeming blood of Jesus, demands that we answer with our best and highest love in return, and this is the Law of Grace.

Logic – That branch of Philosophy which is dedicated to deductive reasoning. Logic is often expressed in phrases such as, " If this, then that." Mathematics, if it were still a philosophical discipline, would fall within Logic. Socrates is regarded as the Father of Logic, for his careful process of reasoning.

Malleable – Capable of being shaped. Malleable metals can be hammered into a shape. Malleable morals can be bent so that any sin can be justified.

Matthew Henry – An 18th century clergyman and theologian. Henry's Commentary on the Whole Bible is widely considered the best Protestant/Non-conformist commentary.

Meaning of Life – The philosophical purpose for which human life exists; the highest Good; the Summum Bonum; the purpose; the reason; the only thing that's not striving after the wind. (hint: It's serving God.)

Mercy – When we deserve something bad, but don't get it, we have tasted Mercy. Mercy goes together with Grace. In Romans 6:23 we learn that the wages of sin is death, but that the Gift of God is Eternal life with Him through Jesus' sacrifice for us. That we don't get spiritual death is God's Mercy; that we can spend eternity with God is God's Grace.

Metafictional Metaphor – Seriously, you looked that up? I only stuck that into the introduction to make the point that some folks get hung up on the pseudo-intellectual baloney and skip the obviously important thoughts directly in front of them. If you really want to know, metafiction is a form of fiction where the writer keeps breaking you out of the plot and reminding you that you're reading a book. If there's a metaphor in a metafictional work, it's a metafictional metaphor.

Metaphor – A stylistic device used to explain a difficult idea by comparing it to something else. If we say, "The general stood like a rock," we are using the firmness of a rock (which everyone understands) to explain the General's bravery under enemy fire (which may not be easily understood by those who did not see it).

Metaphysics – From the Greek, literally meaning "Beyond the physical," Metaphysics is that branch of Philosophy which concerns itself with the supernatural. Theology in its entirety fits within the Metaphysics branch of Philosophy.

Modus Ponens – A form of argument which denies the second clause of a general premise.

Modus Tollens – A form of argument which affirms the first clause of a general premise.

Moot – Not affecting the conclusion, not important to the discussion, irrelevant. Having no force or effect.

Morals, Morality – Morality literally means a following of rules. The idea is that our society has adopted certain rules by which people ought to behave, and those who follow those rules are moral; those who defy them are immoral. Typically, social "mores" involve following the Ten Commandments and maintaining sobriety. People sometimes assume that Jesus taught people to be moral, but in fact Jesus showed the flaws of first-century morality, and called for people to obey a higher law – the Law of Grace.

Mother Kirk – A name that C. S. Lewis used to symbolize the Church.

Myth of the Cave – a concept taught by Socrates, and recorded by Plato: Imagine that prisoners were kept in a cave, such that they could only see a wall of the cave. Behind them, their captors carried shapes of objects in front of a large fire, casting shadows onto the wall. The prisoners believed these shadows to be real. The myth supposes that one prisoner escapes and discovers real trees, real clouds, real animals, and real rain, before being captured and placed back in the cave. On reporting his findings to the other prisoners, he is killed in a fit of their rage. The Myth of the Cave is often compared to the statement by Paul the Apostle, in 1 Corinthians chapter 13, "Now we see through a mirror, darkly, but then face to face; and we shall know as we are known."

Nicodemus – A Jewish leader and a member of the Sanhedrin, who became a secret follower of Jesus. See John 3. Also, one of the two men who acquired Jesus' body after the crucifixion, to bury it.

Nomenclature – The naming of things.

Non-conformist – Someone who doesn't fit the pattern. In Christianity, a Non-conformist is someone who does not conform a certain creed, especially someone who is neither Catholic nor Protestant. Technically, Protestant denominations are a reformation of the Roman Catholic Church, but there are some denominations which were never part of it, and thus could not reform from it. These are best referred to as "Non-conformists." Piedmontese, Anabaptists, and others tend to claim a non-conformist heritage.

Noumena – Things that cannot be known or observed; that which is beyond the limits of human knowledge (Kant).

Novice – Someone who is new to something, especially a religious order or religious studies.

Numinous – Having to do with the mystically spiritual or the spiritual; Eerie; Uncanny.

Ontology – The study of the nature of existence. Also Ontological.

Parsimony – Keeping it simple. The so-called Law of parsimony, or Occam's Razor, says that one should keep one's philosophies simple and elegant. Keep in mind that this is a guiding principle – a simpler idea is more likely to be correct, but is not guaranteed to be correct. Parsimony literally means "Stinginess," as in that we should be stingy with our assumptions and other "entities."

Paul E. Little –- Author of *Know What You Believe*, a guide to Christian doctrines of various denominations.

Paul the Apostle – A former student of Gamaliel, and a fervent defender of Judaism against the encroachment of Christianity, later a convert and eventually an apostle of Christ. Paul was the first Christian missionary, and wrote most of the New Testament.

Phenomena – Events that are observed or observable; Also, things that can be known (Kant).

Philosophy – From the Greek phrase ***Philos Sophia*** (Love of Wisdom), Philosophy is the love of Wisdom. In Classical Times, Philosophy included science, and was the accumulated knowledge and wisdom of that day. Philosophy presently includes disciplines such as Logic, Ethics, Aesthetics, Metaphysics and Epistemology.

Piety – Reverence, respect, or obligation for God or for one's family. In Plato's Euthyphro, Socrates confronts Euthyphro for failing in his Filial Piety (Reverence towards his family).

Plato – A philosopher, and the student of Socrates who recorded Socrates' dialogs. Most ideas which are referred to as "Platonic" actually originate with Socrates, but are known only by the records of Plato. Plato is known for "Platonic Love" (love that has no "romantic" or sexual element), Plato's "Myth of the Cave," and Platonism, which is the idea that there is a deeper and stronger reality, of which our world is a pale shadow. Teacher of Aristotle.

Platonism – The idea, suggested by the Myth of the Cave, that the apparent world has a deeper reality beyond it. Neo-platonism is the idea that the deeper reality is Heaven. C.S. Lewis was a proponent of Neo-platonism.

Postmodernism – The philosophical, artistic, and stylistic fashion that followed modernism. Modernism was an artistic style in the mid to late 20th century, which can be summarized as a rejection of tradition in favor of "Modern" tastes and styles. Post-modernism includes the residue and left-overs of modernism, such as the general belief that new concepts are superior to traditional ideas, or that spiritual traditions are mere superstitions and are irrational.

Prayer – A conversation with God. Prayer can be formal, informal, long, short, calm, or passionate. Whichever it is, God would like to hear from you. Today, if that fits your schedule.

Premise – A foundational step in an argument. Syllogisms use two premises and a set of rules to draw a conclusion.

Prescribe – To recommend or order, especially as a cure or remedy.

Prodigal – Having turned away from the truth or from moral good. Typically used in reference to Jesus' parable of the prodigal son, who was gladly received back by his father, when he repented and returned home.

Profession of Faith – A public statement declaring that one has faith in Jesus Christ. See Romans 10:9-10; compare Peter's spontaneous statement in Matthew 16:16.

Proscribe – To forbid or to order something not to be done.

Pseudonym – An assumed name or "nom-de-plume."

QED, *Quod Erat Demonstratum* – "That which was to be proven," or, more loosely translated, "And that proves my point." Looser still, "So there" or "Nanny-nanny-boo-boo" are possible translations, though they're quite a reach. In general, to add QED on the end of an argument is to suggest that nothing more need be said, and that the matter should be settled, since the question has been answered definitively.

Question – A query, or a matter under debate. "To be or not to be, that is the question…" (Shakespeare, Hamlet).

Reconcile – To bring facts into harmony; to resolve a difference or to settle an argument. The word suggests accounting and bookkeeping; settling the accounts; it can also be used with regard to the restoration of a relationship.

Redeem – To buy back, or to retrieve from a state of forfeiture. In the Old Testament, family members were permitted to buy back lost property every seventh year. The book of Ruth hinges upon redemption by a Kinsman. This is a symbol – a "type"—of how Jesus redeems us from our sin.

Relevant – Having to do with the matter being discussed, pertinent, apropos, on the topic.

Reverent – Respectful. God deserves reverence.

Revelation – A fact or event revealed by God to a person. Also, the name of a book written by John the Disciple, a/k/a John the Revelator, a/k/a John the Elder.

Rhetoric – The art of speaking or of argument. Logic is about the substance of an argument, while rhetoric is about how nice the words of the argument sound to the listener. Rhetoric is style in language; using words that suggest the right idea in the listener's mind, in just the right way. Sometimes a Sophist will use rhetorical style to hide a weak argument, which is why it is important to look for the logic beneath the style.

Rhetorical Question – A question not meant to be answered, and which is asked merely to introduce an idea or an argument. When Juliet asks, "Wherefore art thou Romeo?" she does not intend for him to explain his family name; she merely wants to show that she wishes he belonged to a more compatible family.

Righteousness – The state of being morally and ethically right. As a human pursuit, it is unattainable, but it is given freely by God to those who hunger and thirst for it.

Roman Road – A set of Bible verses, all from the book of Romans, which lead to personal salvation. Romans 3:23, Romans 6:23, Romans 5:8, and Romans 10:9 provide a basic step-by-step plan of salvation: All have sinned; sin leads to death (hell); God loves us despite our sin; and if we confess Jesus as our Lord, believing that God raised Him from the dead, we can be saved from the penalty of our sins.

Salvation – Being saved. In this context, being saved from the penalty of our own sins.

Sanctification – The process by which believers are made Holy, over time, as they learn to defeat the power of sin in their lives.

Scientific Method, the – A reasoning tool consisting of five steps: Defining the question to be answered, Gathering information, Forming a hypothesis, Testing the hypothesis, and Drawing a conclusion.

Sect of the Way – An early description of Christianity, which was initially considered a strange sect of Judaism. It draws its name from the fact that Jesus called Himself "The Way, the Truth, and the Life" (John 14:6)

Security of the Believer – The doctrine that salvation establishes a permanent and unbreakable relationship with God.

Sin – Doing what is wrong in the eyes of God.

Sincere – Without deception, sarcasm, or hidden intention; honest.

Socrates – A philosopher, and the father of Logic. Socrates enjoyed arguing with sophists, getting drunk at parties, and long walks on the beach. Okay, the beach part was never proven. Socrates never lost an argument, including the argument for his life, when he was put on trial for impiety, corrupting the youth, and causing false things to appear to be true. Sure, he was convicted and sentenced to drink hemlock, but people remember his argument, and have forgotten the arguments of the prosecutors.

Socratic Inquiry; Socratic Method – Argument by asking a series of questions, which are designed to lead a listener to the desired conclusion. This method is named for Socrates, because he is the best and first-known example of this style. The weakness of Socratic Inquiry is that it assumes that the Listener will respond in the desired manner.

Sophist, Sophistry – Sophistry is false philosophy or false reasoning, especially that of the Sophists. Sophists were early philosophers who specialized in specious arguments and tricks of pseudo-logic. Socrates spent much of his time deflating sophists. Call them "wise-guys."

Specific Premise – In a syllogism, the second premise, which either affirms the first clause of the general premise, or denies the second clause of the general premise.

Summum Bonum – The sum of all good things; the meaning of life. (Hint: it's serving God).

Supernatural – Literally, "More than natural" or "Above the natural." Spiritual matters are "Supernatural" to the human mind; though one imagines that they are simply "Natural" to God, who created nature.

Syllogism – A logical process invented by Aristotle. Two premises are combined to create a conclusion that "follows" from the premises. These use one of two methods, modus ponens or modus tollens; that is, affirming the first clause of the general premise, or denying the second clause of general premise.

Tabernacle – A tent used for religious meetings, especially for the purpose of being in the presence of God, most especially that tent carried by the Israelites during the exodus from Egypt, above which God was present in the form of a pillar of cloud and of fire. A parallel is drawn in John 1:14, in which we are told that Jesus "dwelt" among us (literally "pitched His tent among us") which is intended to parallel the physical presence of Jesus with the presence of God above the tabernacle of meeting, in the wilderness.

Tanakh – A Hebrew acronym and abbreviation meaning, "The Law, the Prophets, and the Writings." These are the books which Christians refer to as the Old Testament. One might also refer to it as the "Old Covenant."

Tangible – Capable of being touched, sensible, physical.

Tertium Quid – The third thing, or a standard against which to measure or compare other standards. A ruler cannot be used to measure itself, and if two rulers should disagree, there is no obvious way to know which, if either, is right. To know the answer requires a third, more authoritative, measure: The tertium quid.

Testimony – A statement of facts known to the one who testifies; The statement of a witness to an event or a fact. In a religious context, the explanation of one's life before Christ, one's own direct interactions with Christ, and one's life after meeting Christ. It is sometimes misused in certain circles to mean an irrational assurance of things that one cannot directly know, based upon a "burning in the bosom" feeling.

Theology – From the Greek words Theos and Logos, literally "Words about God." Theology in its broad scope is the study of all religion; in the intermediate scope, the study of Christianity, and in its narrow scope, the study of the Christian God. Theology in the intermediate scope includes Theology Proper (study of God the Father), Christology (study of Christ), Pneumatology (study of the Holy Spirit), Angelology (study of angels), Soteriology (study of salvation), Hamartology (study of sin) and Eschatology (study of last things).

Transgressions – One of two categories of sins mentioned in the Bible. Transgression means a crossing of a line or the violation of a boundary. See also, Iniquity.

Unexcluded Middle – There may be more than two choices. For example, if we are asked "What topping did you have on your pizza: Pepperoni or Pineapple?" then we have been presented a false set of choices (a "false dichotomy") because there is an unexcluded middle: We may have chosen sausage, canadian bacon, olives, mushrooms, spinach leaf, green peppers, red peppers, jalapenos, or many other toppings. If a choice can be answered with "both" or "neither" then there is an unexcluded middle, and the choice is a false dichotomy.

Universalism – The belief that everyone will eventually get into heaven, regardless of whether or not they were Christians. This belief is not supported by Scripture.

William of Ockham – The father of Parsimony, who is believed to have said, "Do not multiply entities needlessly," which is sometimes called, "The Law of Parsimony" or "Ockham's Razor." It's not actually in any of his writings, so far as anyone can cite, but it's probably something he said, and it's a good principle to follow. Parsimony, of course, neglects that sometimes the correct answer really is more complicated that the other possible answers.

Woman at the Well – A woman mentioned, but not named, who encountered Jesus at a well in Samaria. See John 4. Of particular note in this passage is the moral imperative in 4:1 (Jesus "must needs" pass through Samaria), the persistence of Jesus in bringing the conversation to spiritual things, the statement about God in 4:24, and Jesus' confession of Deity in 4:26.

Yeshua, Y'shua HaMaschiah – Hebrew name of Jesus, Jesus the Messiah.

Zeitgeist – Literally, the "Spirit of the Age." Zeitgeist is usually used to refer to the currently fashionable concept.

80 Eridani – A star that is between 5 and 7 light-years from Earth. Also the star most similar to the Star Trek star "Vulcan."

APPENDIX A

Syllogisms

Syllogisms consist of three parts: A general premise, a specific premise and a conclusion.

The General premise is often phrased "If A, then B." It can also be phrased, "All A are B" or "B is necessary for A." Thinking of the idea in its' "If A, then B" form will make it easiest to work with.

The Specific premise is a simpler idea which either affirms A, or denies B. To affirm A is called Modus Tollens, and to deny B is called Modus Ponens.

The conclusion is then that portion of the General premise that is not addressed by the Specific premise.

General Premise: If A, then B.
Specific Premise: A.
Conclusion: Therefore B. (***modus tollens***)

Or

General Premise: If A, then B.
Specific Premise: Not B.
Conclusion: Therefore Not A. (***modus ponens***)

All syllogistic arguments take one of these two forms, and virtually any valid argument at all can be shaped into one of these two forms. If any argument cannot be shaped into one of these two forms, the argument is highly suspect and should be re-examined.

"My dog cannot have German Shepherd in its bloodline; German Shepherds all have extra teeth." This argument can be fitted to the modus ponens form:

GP: If a dog is a German Shepherd mix, it will have extra teeth.
SP: This dog does not have extra teeth.
C: Therefore this is not a German Shepherd mix (modus ponens).

If an argument fits the form of either modus ponens or modus tollens, we say that it "follows." This is one of the three tests we apply to an argument:

1: Does it "follow?"
2: Are the premises true?
3: Does each word mean exactly one thing?

In this case, the error is in the second premise: Shepherd mixes do not have extra teeth.

We might also see an argument like this one, used by the sophists:

Sophist: Do you own a dog?
Victim: Yes.
Sophist: Is it a father?
Victim: Yes, it has fathered puppies.
Sophist: It is a father, and it is yours, therefore it is your father, and the puppies are your brothers.
Pressing this into a Syllogistic form, we find:
GP: If you own a father, then it is your father.
SP: Your dog is a father.
C: Therefore your dog is your father.

This fails test 3: The word "your" is used two ways: To indicate ownership (your dog) and to indicate relationship (your father). Thus, it is an ambiguous definition. It also ambiguously defines father, using it to fit both the dog and the man who raised you.

A proper syllogism must:
1. Follow logically (*modus tollens* or *modus ponens*),
2. Have true premises, and
3. Use every word to mean exactly one thing.

A Proper syllogism has:
1. A general premise, usually phrased "if…, then …"
2. A specific premise, which
    2a. affirms the first clause of the general premise, or
    2b. denies the second clause of the general premise, and
3. A conclusion, based on the premises:

3a. If the specific premise is like 2a., then the second clause of the general premise is true.

3b. If the specific premise is like 2b., then the first clause of the general premise is false.

APPENDIX B

An Outline of the Bible

I. Garden:
    A. God created everything from nothing.
    B. God created Man and Woman.
    C. Mankind sinned against God.
    D. God began the long process of redemption.

II. Flood:
    A. Mankind became so evil that God decided to destroy them all and start over.
    B. Noah tried to follow God, so God chose to rescue him and his family.
    C. Noah built an ark on God's instruction, and rescued two of each animal.

III. Abraham:
    A. God spoke to Abraham, a man in Mesopotamia, and sent him across the desert with his clan.
    B. When Abraham reached modern day Israel, God promised it to Abraham's descendants.
    C. Abraham had a son, Isaac.
    D. Isaac had two sons, Esau and Jacob.
    E. Jacob had twelve sons by four wives.

F. Jacob's favorite son, Joseph, the older son of his favorite wife, was hated by the other brothers. They faked his death and sold him into slavery.

G. Joseph worked his way up, and with God's help became the third highest-ranking person in Egypt, responsible for storage and distribution of grain.

H. Jacob and his family endured famine in Canaan. Jacob sent his sons to Egypt to buy grain.

I. Joseph was reconciled with his brothers, and called them all down into Egypt, where they lived in the Nile delta (Goshen). *

IV. Exodus and Journey to Canaan:

A. There arose a Pharaoh who did not remember Joseph. He enslaved the Hebrews, and ordered that male Hebrew babies be killed at birth.

B. Moses was born, a Hebrew. When his parents could hide him no longer, they put him in a basket of reeds and set him adrift on the Nile. He was found and raised by Pharaoh's sister.

C. Moses became aware of his Hebrew heritage. One day, on seeing a Hebrew beaten by an Egyptian, he killed the Egyptian.

D. Moses hid from justice in the barren deserts. There he married and became a shepherd.

E. One day, while watching flocks, Moses discovered a bush, on fire but not burned up. As he approached it, God spoke to him. God instructed Moses to return to Egypt and to free the Hebrew slaves, leading them to Canaan (Modern Israel).

F. Pharaoh was not willing to release the Hebrews, so God used ten plagues to persuade him. When Pharaoh changed his mind and chased Moses, God opened the Red Sea for their escape, then closed it onto the Egyptians.

G. Moses led the people first to the place where he had seen the burning bush. There, he received the ten commandments, which he showed to the people.

H. The Israelites began a long trip to the Promised Land. The tent of God's presence (the tabernacle, or place of worship) was always in the center of the camp. God was with them, "pitching His tent" among them.

I. After a long trip with many adventures, The Israelites reached the border of Canaan. They sent twelve spies. Ten spies gave a pessimistic report. Two gave a positive report.

J. Because they refused to go, Israel wandered in the desert for forty years, until a new generation, willing to go, arose.

K. Moses died, and Joshua took leadership of the nation.**

V. Conquest and Judges:

A. Israel began to conquer Canaan, under Joshua's leadership. They subdued most of the land, but did not completely wipe out the prior residents.

B. After Joshua died, a pattern of behavior began:

1. Israel would begin to fall away from God and worship idols.

2. God would bring judgement or oppression upon them.

3. The people would repent.

4. God would bring a Judge, who would free them.

5. When the judge died, the cycle would repeat.

C. The last Judge, Samuel, appointed the first King, Saul.

VI. United Kingdom:

A. Saul reigned, but did evil before God. God shunned him and had Samuel anoint David, a shepherd boy, to be the next king.

B. Saul tried to have David killed, but eventually died.

C. David became King. He was a great general and a wise leader. This is considered Israel's Golden Age.

D. David sinned and tried to cover it up with murder. God judged the nation and David's family as a result. David repented.

E. After David's death, Solomon became king. He began as a wise king, but fell into idolatry as a result of political marriages.

F. Solomon built Solomon's Temple, the first of three temples to the Hebrew God.

VII. Divided Kingdom:

A. Following Solomon's death, the ten northern tribes broke away from the two southern tribes. The North was called Israel, and the South, Judah.

B. The kings of Israel and of Judah led the people through cycles similar to the pattern of the Judges. Slowly, the kings became more and more corrupt.

C. In time, God permitted Israel to be conquered by the Assyrian Empire. This was the Assyrian Captivity.

D. The ten northern tribes intermarried with the Assyrians, and lost their identity as a people. The New Testament Samaritans were descendants of these mixed marriages.

E. Babylon conquered Assyria.

F. In time, God permitted Judah to be conquered by the Babylonian empire ruled by Nebuchadnezzar. This was the Babylonian Captivity. Jews did not intermarry, and kept their cultural identity.

G. Later, some of the Jews were allowed to return and rebuild Jerusalem. This was when the second of the three temples was built.

H. Eventually the Jews were all allowed to return from Babylon.***

VIII. Jesus' Ministry

A. 483 years after the second temple was built, Jesus was born to a virgin from the tribe of Judah.

B. When He was about 30 years old, He began to work miracles and to preach that the Messiah (the savior) had come.

C. Jesus claimed to be the messiah and the only Son of God.

D. When He was about 33 years old, Jesus was executed on false charges of blasphemy and of insurrection against Rome.

E. Jesus died for the sins of all mankind, and was buried.

F. Jesus rose again on the third day.

G. Jesus was seen by many, including his surviving disciples (Judas had hanged himself).

H. Jesus ascended bodily into heaven.

IX. Church Age

A. Fifty days after Jesus was killed, the assembled disciples and believers were filled with the holy Spirit and began to preach. 3000 Jews were converted that day.

B. The church began to grow, and underwent persecution by the Jews.

C. The first deacon, Stephen, was martyred after preaching to the Pharisees.

D. Saul converted to Christianity after being blinded on the road to Damascus.

E. Peter saw a vision which instructed him to preach to Gentiles. He went with Cornelius to Antioch. A religious awakening began.

F. The church at Jerusalem sent Barnabus to find out what was happening at Antioch. He took Saul, who was now called Paul.

G. As a result of the gospel spreading to the gentiles at Antioch, Paul and Barnabus began a series of missionary journeys to Turkey, Greece, and Eastern Europe.

H. Paul was arrested because of a disturbance at Jerusalem. As a Roman Citizen, he appealed unto Caesar. He was taken to Rome. Along the route, Paul continued to spread the gospel.

I. Paul wrote a series of letters to various churches about religious matters. These letters form the majority of the New Testament.

J. The Apostle John was exiled at Patmos. There he saw a vision of the end times.

X. Future Events:

A. At an unknown date in the future, Jesus Christ will return suddenly and unexpectedly to reclaim His bride, which is the Church.

Second Edition / Third Printing
(First Printing of the Second Edition)

www.ingramcontent.com/pod-product-compliance
Lightning Source LLC
Chambersburg PA
CBHW061429040426
42450CB00007B/969